DRAWN to CHANGE the WORLD

"I just wish someone had told you your true extent.
How you connect to mountain glaciers and tropical orchids.
How you come from ancient fish and before that single cells
that found advantages together. How starlight,
even now, animates everything about you."

—Dr. Elizabeth Sawin

Biologist, climate change researcher, and
cofounder of Climate Interactive

"There is a vision of my community called Kawsak Sacha, which
means 'the Living Forest.' We see us and what surrounds us as
equals, or rather, that we are a part of nature."

—Sumak Helena Sirén Gualinga

Ecuadorean Indigenous advocate for climate justice and cofounder of
Polluters Out, a youth-led campaign to remove the fossil fuel industry's
influence on society

"We need to have a whole cultural shift,
where it becomes our culture to take care of the earth,
and in order to make this shift, we need storytelling about how the
earth takes care of us and how we can take care of her."

—Ayana Elizabeth Johnson

Marine biologist, policy expert, writer & conservation strategist,
from *All We Can Save: Truth, Courage, and Solutions for the Climate Crisis*

"We need to safeguard nature as if our lives depend on it,
because they do. We are nature, defending itself."

—Matthew Shribman

Scientist, environmentalist, and cofounder of AimHi Earth

GRAPHIC NOVEL COLLECTION

DRAWN to CHANGE THE WORLD

16 YOUTH CLIMATE ACTIVISTS, 16 ARTISTS

EMMA REYNOLDS

HARPER alley

An Imprint of HarperCollinsPublishers

HarperAlley is an imprint of HarperCollins Publishers.

Drawn to Change the World Graphic Novel Collection
Text and Introduction copyright © 2023 by Emma Reynolds
Introduction copyright © 2023 by Matthew Shribman
Illustrations on pages 2–5 copyright © 2023 by Natasha Donovan
Illustrations on pages 10–13 copyright © 2023 by Gloria Félix
Illustrations on pages 18–21 copyright © 2023 by Ann Maulina
Illustrations on pages 26–29 copyright © 2023 by Bill Masuku
Illustrations on pages 34–37 copyright © 2023 by Teo DuVall
Illustrations on pages 42–45 copyright © 2023 by Derick Brooks
Illustrations on pages 50–55 copyright © 2023 by Emma Reynolds
Illustrations on pages 60–63 copyright © 2023 by Shivana Sookdeo
Illustrations on pages 68–71 copyright © 2023 by Devon Holzwarth
Illustrations on pages 76–79 copyright © 2023 by Anoosha Syed
Illustrations on pages 84–87 copyright © 2023 by Erin Hunting
Illustrations on pages 92–95 copyright © 2023 by Margarita Kukhtina
Illustrations on pages 100–103 copyright © 2023 by Jade Zhang
Illustrations on pages 108–111 copyright © 2023 by Natasha Nayo
Illustrations on pages 116–119 copyright © 2023 by Victoria Maderna
Illustrations on pages 116–119 copyright © 2023 by Federico Piatti
Essay copyright © 2023 by Jamie Margolin
Interview copyright © 2023 by Emma Reynolds

Library of Congress Control Number: 2022948037
ISBN 978-0-06-308421-6 (pbk.) — ISBN 978-0-06-308422-3

Emma Reynolds used Procreate and Adobe Photoshop to create the illustrations
for this book. The other artists used a combination of digital and non-digital tools,
including Procreate, Adobe Photoshop, gouache paint, and colored pencils.
Typography by Kathy Lam
23 24 25 26 27   GPS   10 9 8 7 6 5 4 3 2 1
First Edition

DEDICATED IN LOVING MEMORY OF ANNA AND NANNY.
Anna—a glittering, wild-haired star
Nanny—knitting and watching the birds
under the blossom from the stars

My heart-filled thank-you to Gray, my friends, and my family for your love and support through the hardest and most challenging years. Anna Terreros-Martin, Mal Razik, Sydni Gregg, and Kelly Leigh Miller—our daily chats and friendship got me through lockdown and beyond. Mountain of thank-yous to Megan Ilnitzki, my amazing editor, who had the vision to ask for this book as a graphic novel and believed in this idea from the start. To my steadfast agent, Thao Le, who always has my back. To Amy Ryan and Kathy Lam for their wonderful design work, and to all the HarperAlley team who work tirelessly behind the scenes making the book the very best it can be.

Special thank-you to all the phenomenal artists and writers who worked so hard with us on this book; I'm so honored I got to work with you, truly. World of thank-yous to the activists in this book; it has been an honor to share your stories in graphic novel form.

To all climate justice activists, and to you, the reader: this book is for you.

Thank you for reading it,
Emma x

TABLE OF CONTENTS

ABOUT THIS BOOK

How #KidLit4Climate began

I was walking through Manchester, UK, on a February 2019 morning in temperatures we normally only experience in the summer, and I thought, *When am I going to do something?*

I didn't want to look back and wish I had done something sooner.

It might be hard to imagine now, but back then, the youth climate strikes had just started to spread farther across Europe and make headlines. But it wasn't in a positive light at first. I distinctly remember a video of a grown man shouting at a young girl for striking from school, and her standing her ground—it angered me to see young people not being taken seriously.

Thinking about what I could do within my field to make a difference, I went to the gym and I had an epiphany on the treadmill. I thought, *I spend all day creating books for children and young people, and if we can't support them as authors and illustrators, then what are we even doing?*

I went home and made the #KidLit4Climate campaign and set up the socials in a flurry of inspiration in a few hours. I should have been doing other deadline work! Instead I drew the logo and put a brief online for people to draw a protestor in solidarity with the youth climate strikes.

I thought I'd maybe get about thirty illustrations sent to me, and I was going to put them in one big image together for the first Global Climate Strike. But the campaign went viral and absolutely exploded—within two weeks I'd been sent one thousand illustrations. A few months and then years later and there are countless thousands of illustrations from over fifty countries around the world in every continent, even Antarctica.

It became the first global illustrated climate campaign. And in the last couple of years we have seen an explosion in climate literature.

I continue to be so in awe of all the incredible illustrators and authors who have taken part in the campaign. It introduced me to many amazing artists too, and I am so happy to say that some of them have worked on this book you are about to read.

Drawn to Change the World

I started working on this book in the pandemic in 2020. Since then, where I am from in the UK has changed. We have experienced the hottest day ever recorded here. Day by day, the country I was born in is becoming more like the countries I wrote about in this book that struggle to protest because of their government and police.

As the corrupt UK Tory government has been breaking international law, decimating vulnerable communities, destroying nature, and pushing more people into poverty, there has also been a suppression of access to information.

They have closed over eight hundred libraries in the last 10+ years, severely cut university funding for creative courses, leading many to stop running, and passed a shocking and draconian policing bill effectively banning peaceful protest.

So it has become even more meaningful that I worked on this book now that we cannot freely peacefully protest here in the streets. But we can in a book.

"Books are a form of political action.
Books are knowledge. Books are reflection.
Books change your mind."
—Toni Morrison

"Art plays a critical role in radical imagination.
Art has the power to bring alive a collective voice."
—intersectionalenvironmentalist.com

It is more important than ever to use our voices and our strengths and join as communities to make change, even when those in power don't want us to do so.

We must continue to peacefully protest wherever and however we can. We must fight book bans in the US and beyond that seek to censor marginalized people's existence. We must demand climate justice and the protection and restoration of nature. We must use our skills and voices as storytellers to help others imagine a transformed future. All while remembering that we humans are part of nature too, not separate from it. We are all one.

This book is not about putting the sole responsibility on young people's shoulders to fix this crisis. It's about celebrating the activists who are doing incredible things, and encouraging whoever is reading this book that you can make a difference too, no matter your age. You are not too old, and you are not too young, to begin. This crisis has been caused by multiple harmful systems that need dismantling—systems led by the super-rich and a few very powerful people and companies. By working as communities and empowering others through climate education, we can work together toward a more equitable, transformed future for us all.

I am so happy we got to make this book to celebrate the youth climate activists who #KidLit4Climate was created for, people who are changing our world for the better. To share their stories, and to inspire others to join them in our collective purpose. To join them in their hopes and dreams of a better world.

Art and books are a protest. This book is a protest.

Thank you so much to everyone who helped create this book with me. And thank you for reading it.

—Emma

EMMA REYNOLDS

is an illustrator and author based in Manchester, UK. Emma started #KidLit4Climate, the first global illustrated climate campaign, in early 2019, bringing together thousands of children's illustrators and authors from more than fifty countries in solidarity with the youth climate strikes. Her author-illustrator debut picture book, *Amara and the Bats*, about bat conservation, community action, and finding hope, is a JLG Gold Standard Selection, an NSTA Best in STEM book, and an EmpathyLab Read for Empathy Selection. She is passionate about storytelling and making accessible SciComm, and is inspired by nature, animals, adventure, and seeing the magic in the everyday. Visit her at emmareynoldsillustration.com.

INTRODUCTION

"In a world that depends on a great diversity
of living things to function, the traditional idea
that only one of those living things—humans—
should be considered in decision-making
isn't going to work much longer."

—Matthew Shribman
Scientist, environmentalist, and cofounder of AimHi Earth

Something we need to remember every day is that we are a part of nature, not separate from it. If nature thrives, so do we. If nature collapses, so do we.

We are often taught to think that our changing climate is the center of this global crisis, but it's not: it's the collapse of nature.

Why do scientists worry about a rapidly changing climate? We worry because it will adversely affect nature. And we worry about nature because nature is where all our food comes from, the air we breathe, the plants and fungi that give us our medicines, the shade of trees in summer, the smell of eucalyptus, the birds singing in the morning, and more or less everything else worth fighting for on this unique and precious planet.

I want to tell you about the word *Ayni*.

It's a Quechuan word that means "today for you, tomorrow for me."

It underpins the Andean culture of reciprocity; a culture that European colonists took advantage of and then did their best to stamp out.

This same kind of sentiment, of giving being more important than getting, is interwoven into the knowledge and cultures of Indigenous peoples all around the world. It's the key principle that, complemented by their vast knowledge of nature, ensures that these people give to nature as much if not more than they receive from it.

Meanwhile, most of the currently dominant cultures in the world have all but lost this way of living. Instead of giving back to nature, these cultures are pillaging and destroying it like there's no tomorrow . . . an increasingly self-fulfilling prophecy.

It's no wonder that when many of us hear author and educator William A. Ward's quote "Judge each day not by the harvest you reap but by the seeds you plant" we think that it sounds remarkable, rather than obvious and totally inherent to the way we live.

The Indigenous cultures that base their systems of understanding around the notion of reciprocity aren't less dominant because they're less good than our cultures. As the brilliant Wade Davis says: "They are unique expressions of the human imagination and heart, unique answers to a fundamental question: What does it mean to be human and alive?" If anything, these Indigenous cultures are, in many ways, superior to ours, particularly in their ability to retain the health of nature and, in doing so, ensure the long-term habitability of our one and only home.

Which brings me to this graphic novel that you're about to begin.

This book is about the climate and nature crisis, but it's not about what's going wrong—it's about what all of us can do.

But it's also about much more than that. It tells the stories of a bunch of seriously inspiring young people who have already done and are continuing to do so much to fight for your and my future. Some of them I'm lucky to count among my friends, others I'm a fan of, and some I'm just learning about now, perhaps like you.

As you read this, you might consider the notion of reciprocity . . .

In most cases, across the animal and even plant (and probably fungal!) worlds, adults are responsible for the young. Young people accept extraordinary gifts of care and compassion and education such that they can one day reciprocally give these gifts back to the next generation.

It says a lot about the state of our culture and society that our balance of reciprocity is so broken that many of the greatest leaders in the climate movement are young people, rather than adults.

Yes, many of us adults are doing our best to combat the climate and nature crisis, but so many are worsening it— mostly because of a lack of understanding, but worsening it all the same.

So, as you discover the stories of these young people, consider the weight on them, above and beyond the weight of being leaders in a global movement. Consider how much they have sacrificed to try to win back our future, which is in so much jeopardy.

It's inspiring, yes, but it's also heartbreaking. I spent my younger years unworried about the climate and nature crisis, writing and performing music as Ash Lad. I was receiving gifts from the world before I started doing what I'm doing now: giving back as an environmentalist, activist, and science communicator.

Consider that these young people, and countless more like them (perhaps you are one of them, reading this now), deserve not just to win their battles but also to receive a great deal of support from all of us.

So, if this graphic novel doesn't make you want to do something to make a difference, like picking up a placard and joining the peaceful protests pushing for political decisions to be made with nature in mind, with future generations in mind, informed by science, justice, equity, and compassion, rather than greed, selfishness, and power . . . then I don't know what will.

The people of the world are waking up to the unparalleled importance of this movement: to stop fossil fuels, to restore nature, and to save our civilization.

We don't need to be famous or powerful to make a difference. We are not a number on a carbon footprint calculator. We are each a node in an evolving network of humanity. Every decision we make affects the decisions of others. Every positive change we bring about contributes to a growing cascade that will trigger the positive societal tipping points that will stop this crisis in its tracks and turn it around. I hope you'll join us.

Thank you, Emma, and all the other artists for creating this graphic novel. It's an important piece of work. As an environmentalist, I appreciate it enormously, and I hope that if you're about to read it yourself, you will enjoy it too.

In the immortal words of ethologist and conservationist Dr. Jane Goodall: "We all make a difference every day. It's up to each of us to decide what kind of difference that will be."

MATTHEW SHRIBMAN

is a scientist, communicator, and environmentalist focused on projects for the future of life on Earth.

He is a cofounder of AimHi Earth, whose team is racing to ensure everyone understands the climate and nature crisis, what's at stake, and how we can turn the world around together. AimHi Earth sees a future where "nature" has a seat at every boardroom, political, and kitchen table.

Matthew has taught and mentored people all around the world—including Olympic athletes, politicians, climate justice activists, corporate executives, and celebrities—and his online videos have been viewed by millions. He also gave the first ever TEDx Talk from a bathtub, though that's another story!

His environmental work has led to things like a hundred-fold increase in the UK's reforestation plans and numerous institutions dropping beef in favor of plant-based foods.

Matthew also really likes bees.

Put simply, humans burning fossil fuels and destroying nature is causing the earth to heat rapidly. Since the Industrial Revolution, humans began to burn vast amounts of fossil fuels to run machines, power our homes, and fuel our vehicles. Currently in the 2020s, we are using more fossil fuels faster than ever before.

In the last one hundred years, Earth's heat has increased by about 1.2 degrees Celsius. That doesn't sound like much, but it's already having devastating global effects such as extreme weather and uninhabitable heat, drought, and flooding. This affects absolutely everything from food production and water access, to people becoming climate refugees and more animals being pushed to extinction. This is why it's so important we do everything possible as a species to limit global heating as much as we can, as quickly as we can.

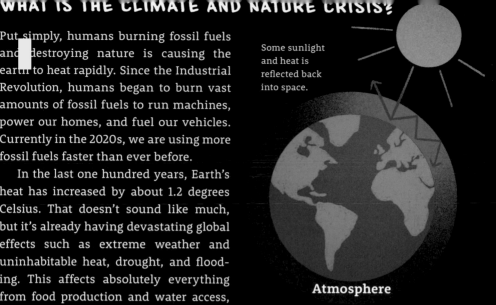

Some sunlight and heat is reflected back into space.

Atmosphere

Greenhouse gases such as CO_2 trap the heat and it can't escape, causing the earth to warm.

We need the greenhoue effect or we would freeze, but humans are causing the earth to heat *too quickly*.

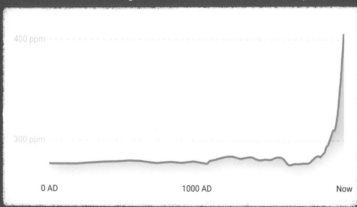

The increase in CO_2 emissions over the last 2,000 years.

400 ppm

300 ppm

0 AD   1000 AD   Now

Graph reproduced with permission of AimHi Earth, using data from co2levels.org/#sources

What percentage of CO_2 has built up in your lifetime?
—AimHi Earth

—If you're 50: 75% of emissions in lifetime
—If you're 30: 50% of emissions in lifetime
—If you're 15: 30% of emissions in lifetime

The speed at which we're releasing greenhouse gases into the atmosphere, which causes the earth to heat up, means our natural "carbon sinks" that absorb CO_2, like trees, can't do their job fast enough. Humans are also rapidly destroying these natural carbon sinks through aggressive deforestation, destruction of healthy topsoil, and the acidification and polluting of our oceans—speeding up global warming even faster.

The solution is already out there and is quite simple— we need to stop using fossil fuels immediately, and protect and restore nature as fast as we can.

The climate and nature crisis doesn't just affect us humans, who have grown accustomed to believing we can just "move somewhere else" or "wear different clothes," because animals don't have this option at all. One million species are on the brink of extinction, and this is happening one thousand times faster than normal. In the last fifty years, we have lost 90 percent of our wild mammals alone. Humans are not separate from nature, we *are* nature, and we rely on it completely to survive. We also need to protect the species that cannot protect themselves.

Who is emitting the most?

Richest 10% = 50% of emissions

Poorest 50% = 10%

Did you know that just 10 percent of the wealthiest people on Earth are responsible for half of global emissions? And the poorest 50 percent of people on Earth only emit 10 percent? Around just 100 companies are responsible for 71 percent of global emissions. It is the wealthiest and most powerful companies that need to change their ways. Blaming population growth is not effective, as not everyone has the same impact.

MORE ABOUT OUR NATURAL CARBON SINKS

Plants and trees

Plants and trees are a natural carbon sink, absorbing CO_2 from the atmosphere and cooling the planet, but they are being cut down at a shockingly fast rate. The biggest cause of deforestation is farming, mostly to grow crops to feed animal livestock. In the Amazon rain forest, an area the size of a football field is cut down every second, and 91 percent of that cleared space is for farming. When trees are then burned, they change from being a carbon sink into a carbon source, emitting CO_2 into the atmosphere rather than capturing it.

Not only is this heating the earth, but wild animals are also losing their habitats and being pushed to extinction, and the potential for human medicines found naturally in the wild is being lost.

Soil

Did you know that soil is actually alive?

"One teaspoon of healthy soil contains more living things than there are members of the human race!"
—Matthew Shribman

Farmers are under immense pressure to intensively farm the land due to demand. By adding in chemical fertilizers and plowing topsoil, delicate mycelial networks are destroyed and vast amounts of carbon are released. The soil takes hundreds of years to recover fully, but if we support farmers to look after soil more and put it first, our food will have more nutrients, and the healthy soil will have the ability to capture vast amounts of CO_2.

The ocean

The ocean is one of the earth's biggest carbon sinks, mostly thanks to microscopic algae and phytoplankton absorbing about half of the CO_2 on Earth. These tiny beings eat things on the ocean surface, then their excretion sinks and the carbon is captured on the ocean floor. But because of the vast amount of plastic that ends up in the ocean, the phytoplankton are eating the microplastics, meaning their excretion floats more and doesn't sink as quickly, affecting their ability to trap carbon deep in the ocean. Plastic is also getting into the food chain, with the toxins increasing the higher up it goes, eventually being ingested by humans and other animals that eat fish and seafood.

Bottom trawling, the destructive fishing practice of huge nets scraping up everything in their path along the bottom of the ocean, destroys marine life and releases this sunken captured CO_2. This fishing practice has no regulation in deep seas and kills species that humans don't even eat in the process.

The more CO_2 there is in the atmosphere, the more the pH level in the ocean decreases, causing acidification of the oceans—which bleaches coral and makes it difficult for marine organisms to develop and grow.

How this affects the ice caps

When ice caps melt, there is less bright ice reflecting heat, and more dark oceans are exposed and absorbing heat. Melting ice caps also cause sea levels to rise, which will mean some coastal cities and entire island communities will lose their homes underwater.

Farming, land space, and diets

One of the most powerful things we can all do is to shift our diet away from animal products (meat, fish, dairy) to a more plant-based diet. Beef has the biggest land and emissions impact of all.

What about protein?

Most humans eat more protein than they actually need, and plants provide the same protein that cows, pigs, and chickens eat. Eating plants is a much more efficient way of getting the protein we need, and helps the planet too.

For one serving of protein . . .

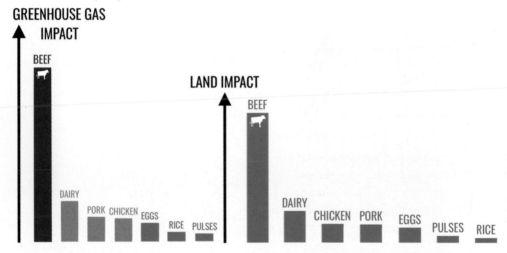

Chart reproduced with permission of AimHi Earth[1]

But is there really enough food to feed everyone?

Yes, there is! But we need to make some changes to our diets, agricultural and farming practices, and reduce food waste. Currently a third of all food is wasted before we can even eat it due to things like high supermarket standards for imperfect shapes and surface marks.

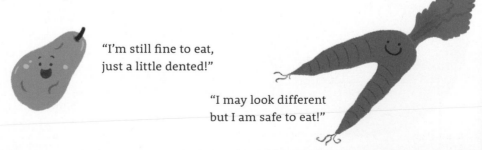

"I'm still fine to eat, just a little dented!"

"I may look different but I am safe to eat!"

Rewilding our world

If we put all the mammals on Earth in big piles, this is what it would look like (the wild mammal percentage is shocking, right?).

Biomass Distribution:

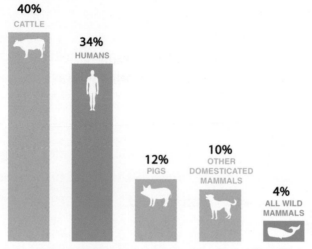

Chart reproduced with permission of AimHi Earth[2]

Let's look at land space. Of the habitable land on earth, only 1 percent is cities. Most of it—50 percent—is used for agriculture, mainly growing crops to feed animals that humans then eat. If we freed up some of this land space from growing crops to feed animals, we could feed humans instead, and use the extra space to rewild the land and help to cool the earth, while restoring habitats for wild animals.

[1] Land & greenhouse gas impact data from wri.org/research/shifting-diets-sustainable-food-future

[2] Biomass data from ourworldindata.org/uploads/2021/03/Distribution-of-earths-mammals.png

WHO IS MOST VULNERABLE
TO CLIMATE CHANGE?

Communities that are already marginalized are the most vulnerable to climate change. That means these people already face discrimination rooted in historical and ongoing systems of oppression.

These marginalized communities include Indigenous peoples, Black communities, people of color, unhoused people, those in poverty, women and girls, LGBTQIA+ people, and disabled people.

Women and girls make up the vast majority of those living in poverty, and 80 percent of people displaced by climate change are women. They are more vulnerable because they are often caregivers, less likely to be in positions of power, more likely to be responsible for food and heat (which they rely on depleting natural resources for), and are more at risk of gender-based violence.

It also matters where you are geographically. People in countries already experiencing extreme heat, drought, and floods are already facing the biggest impacts from climate change yet disproportionately release the least global emissions. Coastal cities and island nations are also the most at risk of rising sea levels.

DID YOU KNOW?

Indigenous peoples make up less than 5 percent of the global population, but they protect 80 percent of the world's biodiversity, as they have lived in balance with the rest of nature for thousands of years.

The people who are the most impacted by climate change need to be part of the decision-making in the climate and nature crisis, with Indigenous peoples at the center.

CANADA

AUTUMN PELTIER

Illustrated by
NATASHA DONOVAN

Autumn grew up by Lake Huron, one of the largest freshwater lakes on earth.

Autumn is 8 years old.

Come on, Autumn, we're going to be late for the water ceremony!

Mom, how far is it to Serpent River?

About an hour and a half. Are you excited?

Yeah!

Say hello to your great-aunt!

Hi, Auntie Josephine! Back in a minute.

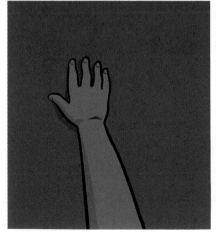

But that's so unfair...

It is... It's very wrong. Your auntie Josephine has been fighting for clean water for a long time.

That's why she was named chief water commissioner, our water protector.

Watch them put the tobacco in the water. They are praying and sending good energy.

Autumn couldn't stop thinking about the contaminated water.

She made up her mind to do something about it.

Autumn started by bringing her message to her school, and in 2014 she was invited to speak at the Children's Climate Conference in Sweden.

Everyone deserves clean drinking water. But our water is sick...

When Autumn was 12, she made headlines worldwide at the 2016 Assembly of First Nations annual winter meeting. She was not given time to give her prepared speech that day, but she confronted the Canadian prime minister, Justin Trudeau, about his approval of two oil pipelines threatening water in native lands.

4

I'm very unhappy about the choices you've made and broken promises to my people.

I understand.

The pipelines...

I will protect the water.

Despite Trudeau's promise, he continued to approve controversial pipelines, with one spilling shortly after.

Don't let anyone stop you.

Everything and everyone needs water.

Mother Earth has been in existence for billions of years and it has only taken us less than a century to destroy her.

Over time, pipelines erode, rot, and break down. They are still polluting our water. It's time for humanity to stop terrorizing Mother Earth and give her time to heal.

Since then, Autumn has spoken all over the world, including at the United Nations General Assembly.

We came together for Standing Rock, and we can certainly come together for water.

In May 2019, Autumn was named the new chief water commissioner for the Anishinabek Nation, after her auntie and mentor Josephine Mandamin passed away.

From 2015–2022, the Canadian government lifted 137 long-term boil advisories. But as of early 2023, 29 communities are still affected by toxic drinking water, and Trudeau continues to invest in pipelines. Autumn has vowed to always fight for clean water all over the world.

5

WHAT ARE THEY DOING NOW?

Autumn is the chief water commissioner of the Anishinabek Nation and is responsible for representing forty First Nations in Ontario, Canada.

President Trudeau has continued to break his promise to Autumn and the Indigenous people, who still do not all have access to clean, safe water. In his 2015 election campaign he vowed to remove all boil water advisories by March 2021. He failed to meet this deadline, while approving controversial pipeline construction and expansions. In June 2020, the Trans Mountain Pipeline had a major spill of almost 200,000 liters of oil, one of more than eighty times it has spilled since being built.

Autumn addressed the United Nations in 2018 and 2019 for the start of the Water Action Decade, an international plan for water conservation and sustainable development. In 2020 she was one of the teenage changemakers at the World Economic Forum in Davos, Switzerland.

She regularly speaks out about environmental racism: where First Nation communities are disproportionately subjected to police violence when protesting, and the contrast of white Canadian people having their clean water needs met immediately. "Indigenous communities are living in third-world-country conditions in a first-world country. It should not be like this."

Autumn has won many awards and honors, including: Sovereign Medal of Exceptional Volunteerism 2017, Ottawa Riverkeeper Award 2018, Environment Award at Racial

Justice Awards 2021, and the Daniel G. Hill Young Leader Award 2022.

In 2020 Autumn featured in the multi-award-winning documentary and animation *The Water Walker*, released in 2022, about her life, roots, passion, and perseverance. Autumn is studying Indigenous politics at college and hopes to become a politician and chief.

"We can't eat money, or drink oil.
One day, I will be an ancestor,
and I want my descendants to know
I used my voice so they could
have a future."
—AUTUMN PELTIER

Born: 2004
Social media:
 @autumn.peltier
 @autumnpeltier1

UNITED STATES

TOKATA

Illustrated by
GLORIA FÉLIX

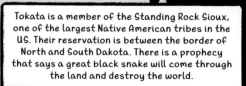

Tokata is a member of the Standing Rock Sioux, one of the largest Native American tribes in the US. Their reservation is between the border of North and South Dakota. There is a prophecy that says a great black snake will come through the land and destroy the world.

Oil pipelines run underground all over the US, transporting oil huge distances. In 2016, the Dakota Access Pipeline (DAPL) was planned to redirect from its route through Bismarck (where the population is mainly white) and instead, cut through the tribe's sacred land and vital water sources. DAPL would transport nearly half a million barrels of oil every day, crossing the Missouri River, which provides drinking water for 28 tribes. Energy Transfer, the company behind the pipeline, have a terrible history of hundreds of leaks and accidents on their other pipelines.

Tokata was 12 years old when she heard about the plan for DAPL. Along with 30 other young people from Standing Rock, she decided to take action, and they formed a youth-led group called ReZpect Our Water.

CANADA
Devils Lake
North Dakota   Fargo
Bismarck
Standing
Rock
Reservation
Rapid City
Sioux Falls
South Dakota
Sioux City

Together with Anna Lee Rain Yellowhammer, Bobbi Jean, and Standing Rock Youth, Tokata started a petition and made a video...

Oil companies keep telling us this is perfectly safe, but we've learned that's a lie: from 2012-13 alone, there were 300 oil pipeline breaks in North Dakota. With such a high chance that this pipeline will leak, I can only guess that the oil industry keeps pushing for it because they don't care about our health and safety.

It's like our lives are more expendable than others'.

They will basically ruin our water source.

The oil will make the animals really sick.

The petition started a powerful movement and gained over half a million signatures. Their video went viral, allowing them to share their message with the world on social media.

Tokata and Native American youth held spiritual relay races, running 30-80 miles every day to complete the 1,200 mile distance between Standing Rock and Washington, DC, to deliver their petitions to lawmakers.

Meanwhile, the Standing Rock Sioux adults were trying their best to stop the pipeline in court. Unfortunately, their first legal battle was defeated. The pipeline company was supposed to check with them and do an environmental impact study to check it was safe, but they didn't, and the permits were approved anyway. Despite breaking federal law and treaties between the US government and Native Americans, the pipeline was approved. Tokata, her friends, and the whole tribe were devastated. So Standing Rock set up "Sacred Stone," their first camp near where DAPL would cross the river so they could protect their water.

Over the next few months, over 10,000 people from more 300 tribes came together in an exceptional movement of unity and solidarity. They set up several spiritual camps near the Missouri River, sharing food, resources, and praying together on the front lines, to peacefully protect their water. Soon, the #NoDAPL movement was making headlines all over the world.

When pipeline construction began in August, thousands of water protectors and allies tried to block it. Police and security became violent against protestors. From August to October, over 260 protestors were arrested. As tensions increased, the water protectors broadcast live on social media what was really happening, shocking people around the globe and encouraging international support.

On December 4, 2016, President Barack Obama announced that DAPL would not be built and construction would stop. Tokata and her friends celebrated this huge victory.

But on February 7, 2017, newly elected President Trump left the Paris Agreement and ordered that DAPL be completed on Native land, as he had personal investments in the pipeline company (which is a conflict of interest and technically illegal!).

The spiritual camps were shut down and the other tribes returned home. The pipeline was finished and delivered its first oil in May 2017.

As expected, within the first 6 months, DAPL already had 5 devastating oil spills.

But Standing Rock didn't let this defeat them. Taking energy and inspiration from the #NoDAPL tribal unity, the Oceti Šakowiŋ (Seven Council Fires) were inspired to work together toward a more sustainable future.

They set up a sustainable energy group called Indigenized Energy Initiative, and Tokata was named one of the board members. In August 2019, nonprofit GivePower and Cody Two Bears of Standing Rock unveiled the very first solar energy farm in North Dakota.

I don't know if you guys know what this means for me right here. It means I get to have a safe future. It means my children get to have a safe future... This is the beginning. I cannot wait to build more of these.

Later that year, Tokata invited Greta Thunberg to speak at her school, before they held a rally together the next day in South Dakota.

Indigenous people have been leading this fight for centuries. They have taken care of the planet and they have lived in balance with nature, and we need to make sure that their voices are being heard.

The 2020 US presidential election saw a historic number of Native American voters, who helped Biden win in key states. On his first day in office, they welcomed his move to rejoin the Paris Agreement and cancel the newly proposed Keystone XL Pipeline from Canada to the US.

We are at the edge of a cliff in regards to our timeline to save this planet, and the Indigenous people will be the ones to lead the movement away from the edge.

Over 400,000 people signed a petition to urge President Biden to also close DAPL, but to people's shock and dismay, in April 2021 the Biden administration decided not to shut it down. The fight continues to close the pipeline.

Tokata will not give up. She continues to travel the world and speak publicly about the uncomfortable truths of Native American oppression and colonization, and how Indigenous solutions are key to solving the climate crisis.

SHUT DOWN DAPL

BIDEN, ARMY CORPS: YOUR INACTION = OUR DEATH

80% of the world's remaining biodiversity is in Indigenous lands. And that's because we've not allowed our lands and our sacred homelands to be desecrated or exploited in the name of economic progress.

VOTE

WHAT ARE THEY DOING NOW?

Tokata first began her activism at age nine in 2013 when she testified against a uranium mine in the Sacred Black Hills.

In May 2019, Tokata was featured in the comic book series Marvel's Hero Project, and on Disney+ in the *Marvel's Hero Project* documentary series in January 2020.

Tokata's main focus with her ongoing activism is LAND-BACK, the reclamation of everything stolen from Indigenous peoples. Their website states:

"LANDBACK is a movement that has existed for generations with a long legacy of organizing and sacrifice to get Indigenous Lands back into Indigenous hands. It allows us to envision a world where Black, Indigenous & POC liberation coexists."

Tokata has been interviewed internationally and uses her platform to stress that Indigenous communities are on the front lines of the climate crisis. She has won several awards, including the Peggy C. Charren Free to Be You and Me Award in 2020, was an International Peace Honoree 2022, and has been featured in several books. Tokata is proudly queer and is a singer and songwriter.

"Wherever we are standing and sitting,
we are connected to everything
that has ever existed and everything that
is to come. We are connected to
every living thing, every plant,
every animal. Acknowledging that,
we realize that we are the same,
that we are one, and that we owe it to
ourselves to be kinder to one another."
—TOKATA

Born: 2004
Website: landback.org

INDONESIA

MELATI
& ISABEL
WIJSEN

Illustrated by
ANN MAULINA

Their classmates joined them, and together they spread the word in the local community.

Thank you so much for your help!

No problem!

In 2014, the sisters wanted to show politicians they were serious and grab media headlines. Inspired by Gandhi, they decided to fast from dawn till dusk. Just two days later, governor of Bali Made Mangku Pastika invited them to meet with him.

Today we promise to work together to reduce plastic pollution in Bali.

A year later, Governor Pastika officially announced his aim for a plastic-free Bali by 2018.

The sisters continued on their mission against plastic, and in 2015 they started a community movement called One Island One Voice, a beach cleanup in Bali, which removes tons of garbage every year.

We want to empower people to do what is right through education, campaigns, and political meetings. Start making that difference one bag at a time.

They made an educational leaflet about plastic pollution to give to schools. By 2016 they had spoken to over 15,000 students in 10 different countries in 5 languages.

In 2016, they gave their second TED Talk, and continued to put pressure on leaders through their campaigns.

Us kids may be only 25% of the world's population, but we are 100% of the future.

After 6 years of hard work, single-use plastics were officially banned in Bali in July 2019!

Bye Bye Plastic Bags is now an international movement, with over 25 locations across the globe. Isabel and Melati continue to share their message around the world.

YOUTHOPIA

In 2020, after 5 years of planning, they founded YOUTHOPIA, a community-centered website with peer-to-peer learning programs and resources, to pass on their activism knowledge and experience to others.

WHAT ARE THEY DOING NOW?

Alongside Bye Bye Plastic Bags and One Island One Voice, in 2017 Melati and Isabel created Mountain Mamas, a social enterprise empowering local women in Bali to produce alternative bags from pre-loved materials, providing women with new skills, flexible working hours, and their own income. With the support of WWF Indonesia, in December 2021 they established another Mountain Mamas in Bogor, Java.

Melati and Isabel have won several prestigious awards, including the Award for Our Earth Bambi Award in 2017 and the Earth Prize in 2020, and have been featured in international press and several books.

In 2018 Melati left high school a year early to focus on being a full-time changemaker. She was named a CNN Hero and a Forbes 30 Under 30. She continues to speak on global stages such as the UN headquarters and has given several TED Talks.

Melati was a presenter in the 2021 documentary feature film *Bigger Than Us*, directed by Flore Vasseur. In the film, Melati travels the world and meets other young activists who are changing and saving lives. It premiered at the Cannes Film Festival and went on to be nominated for a Golden Eye and César Award.

At the World Economic Forum in January 2020, Melati announced the launch of the sisters' new venture and focus with these words: "YOUTHTOPIA is about how we can raise an entire generation of frontline young changemakers . . . We wanted to help empower other young kids around the world to be able to find a tangible action that they could do to equip them with the right tools, the right skills, and the right resources to start making a difference and find their voice as a changemaker."

In early 2023, Isabel graduated as Best Student at Bali Culinary Pastry School.

"We've become literally a living example
that kids *can do things.*
It doesn't matter how old you are,
and it doesn't matter where
you are in the world.
Just find that one thing that you are
passionate about, *and go for it*!"
—MELATI WIJSEN

Born: Melati 2000, Isabel 2002

Website: melatiwijsen.com

byebyeplasticbags.org

youthtopia.world

Social media:

⊡ @isabel.wijsen

⊡ @melatiwijsen

⊡ @youthtopia.world

🐦 @youthtopiaworld

TANZANIA

EDGAR EDMUND TARIMO

Illustrated by
BILL MASUKU

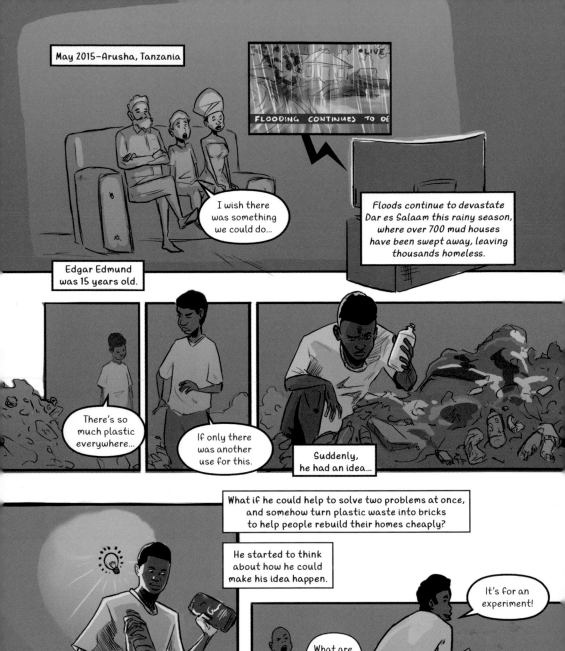

May 2015—Arusha, Tanzania

FLOODING CONTINUES TO DE

I wish there was something we could do...

Floods continue to devastate Dar es Salaam this rainy season, where over 700 mud houses have been swept away, leaving thousands homeless.

Edgar Edmund was 15 years old.

There's so much plastic everywhere...

If only there was another use for this.

Suddenly, he had an idea...

What if he could help to solve two problems at once, and somehow turn plastic waste into bricks to help people rebuild their homes cheaply?

He started to think about how he could make his idea happen.

That summer, he began to collect small bits of plastic.

What are you doing that for?

It's for an experiment!

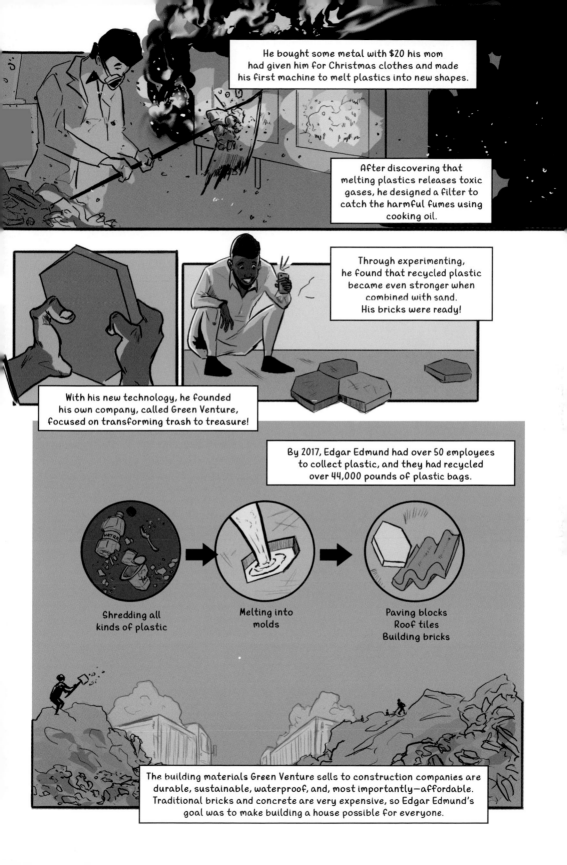

In 2017, Edgar Edmund was first runner-up in the Anzisha Prize, which celebrates innovative young African entrepreneurs. This introduced him to the African Leadership Academy (ALA).

He attended the ALA boot camp, where he gained invaluable skills for running his business and met other networks of people.

That same year, Edgar Edmund was the grand prize winner of the Children's Climate Prize in Sweden.

The jury is full of admiration. With a minimum of resources, Edgar Edmund has shown great entrepreneurship, with astounding knowledge and a marvel of creativity. He has made a great contribution locally and also for the environment and climate on a global scale.

All the finalists are doing great things. We are the product of what surrounds us. So we have to protect the environment and thus it will protect us.

Edgar Edmund went on to win many more awards. He was featured in Forbes Africa Disrupters of 2030, and the BBC made a short film about him.

These opportunities allowed him to expand his business and his team and upgrade his machinery to help even more people. Edgar Edmund also uses his platform to encourage adults to believe in young people.

WHAT ARE THEY DOING NOW?

When Edgar Edmund was in high school, he founded an environmental club to reduce the school's carbon footprint and to encourage students to get involved in campaigns to increase awareness of the climate and nature crisis. He was also a member of the Africamoja Youth Society, where he took part in environmental programs and activities. Edgar Edmund ran environmental programs in other schools too, and has educated over 4,000 students about plastic pollution and climate change.

In 2018, Edgar Edmund gave a speech to over 2,000 people from around 200 countries at the One Young World summit at The Hague in the Netherlands, where he was also able to connect with some of the world's most influential people, such as global activists, inventors, and Nobel Prize winners.

He has received many more honors and awards, including: International Eco-Hero: Outstanding Innovator 2017; Tanzania Youth Innovation 2017: Plastic Recycling; Global Inclusion Awards 2018: Outstanding Youth Economic Citizenship Award.

In 2021, Green Venture Tanzania showcased their work to Samia Suluhu Hassan, the president of Tanzania, and she praised their great work.

Edgar Edmund is currently studying at Whitman College in Washington, US, graduating in 2025. He continues to speak all over the world about his work and the urgent need to reduce plastic pollution.

"By 2050 it's predicted we'll have more plastics than fish in the ocean. And that's what I'm really, really trying to help reduce as much as possible. I believe that when there are a lot of people doing what I do, it can really help reduce plastic pollution in the world."
—EDGAR EDMUND TARIMO

Website: greenventuretanzania.com
Social media:
green_venture_tanzania

UNITED STATES

JAMIE MARGOLIN

Illustrated by
TEO DUVALL

Seattle—2017

How's the Plant-for-the-Planet volunteering going?

You work so hard; pace yourself!

It's going great, thanks! I'm learning so much from everyone. I just...wanna do something to really make leaders wake up to the climate crisis, you know? Something youth-led, like a march. Like the Women's March, and the civil rights youth marches.

Jamie held on to this idea for a while. Later that year, wildfires swept across Canada, covering Seattle in a thick smog.

Hurricanes Harvey, Irma, and Maria devastated communities, and yet the media and leaders still didn't communicate the underlying cause—climate change.

It was then that 15-year-old Jamie decided to put her idea into action.

Jamie made a sign and posted it on social media.

BALTIMORE

Liked by Nadia Nazar and others
Jamie Margolin #YouthMarchOnWashington DM me if you want to join!
Nadia Nazar Count me in!
view all 175 comments

Jamie and Nadia started calling and chatting every day, and became best friends. Soon, Jamie invited her new friends Madelaine Tew and Zanagee Artis to join them, and they founded Zero Hour, their youth-led climate justice movement. They communicated through email, phone calls, and video conferences around school time.

Nadia

Jamie

Zanagee

Madelaine

They worked closely with adult climate justice mentors who helped them build a website and set up fundraising. They connected with more youth who joined the movement, and they spent over a year planning the march.

They planned to march with other groups, including the Sunrise Movement, Indigenous youth from Standing Rock who run #NoDAPL, and many more grassroots organizations.

The four friends finally got to meet in person before the march.

The whole team worked super hard, putting their heart and soul into the final preparations.

We chose our name and logo because it's Zero Hour to act on climate change. There's no more time to wait or deal with it later. This is it!

LOVE YOUR MOTHER

CLIMATE ACTION NOW!!

YOUTH FOR CLIMA

On July 21, 2018, Zero Hour and their ally groups marched in Washington, DC, in a pouring rainstorm, alongside 25 other marches around the world, demanding urgent climate action from their leaders. The Youth Climate March made headlines and helped lay the groundwork for the school strike movement that followed.

Youth all around the world have been marching for a lot longer than this.

Youth, especially youth of color and Indigenous youth, have been raising their voices for climate justice longer than we can count.

In September 2019, before the upcoming United Nations Climate Summit, Jamie testified before the United States Congress alongside fellow youth activists, encouraging leaders to take urgent climate action.

MS. THUNBERG

MS. MARGOLIN

MR. BARRETT

Youth climate activism should not have to exist. We are exhausted because we have tried everything. We've built organizations, organized marches, and worked on political campaigns. How do I even begin to convey to you what it feels like to know that within my lifetime the destruction that we have already seen from the climate crisis will only get worse?

Solving the climate crisis goes against everything that our country was unfortunately built on: colonialism, slavery, and natural resource extraction.

END CLIMATE
COLO...
INDIGENOUS RIGHTS!
LEAVE IT IN THE GROUND
NO PIPELINES

This is why the youth are calling for a new era altogether.

The era of the Green New Deal.

People call my generation "Generation Z" as if we are the last generation. But we are refusing to be the last letter in the alphabet.

YOUTH TO POWER

In 2020, Jamie published her first book, *Youth to Power*, a guide to being an activist with tips to maintain good mental health.

I would tell my younger self to stop thinking that overwork and exhaustion is a badge of honor. It's not.

It's important to look after yourself and make time for things you enjoy outside of your activism too.

I want to tell stories and make films with the representation I wish I'd had growing up.

Jamie continues to use her platform to speak about LGBTQ+ rights and climate justice, and how this intersects with all other forms of social justice, because marginalized groups are affected the most by climate change. Jamie is a proud Latina Jewish lesbian and studied film and television at New York University, creating TV shows about queer youth.

WHAT ARE THEY DOING NOW?

In February 2018, Jamie, twelve other young people, and non-profit Our Children's Trust filed a lawsuit against her home state of Washington for violating the youngest generation's constitutional rights to life, liberty, property, equal protection of the law, and the pursuit of happiness by worsening the climate crisis. The court ruled to dismiss the ongoing case, and Jamie vowed to not stop fighting for climate justice, because it's a matter of survival.

Zero Hour has over 200 chapters worldwide, and continues to be a key part of the climate justice movement—organizing rallies, sharing knowledge, and petitioning governments to stop funding fossil fuels and oil pipelines.

Jamie has written many inspiring articles for magazines and newspapers such as the *New York Times*, *Washington Post*, and *Teen Vogue*, and has spoken to leaders and audiences all over the world. Her honors include being an MTV EMA Generation Change Award winner, being named one of the BBC's 100 most influential women in 2019, and being one of GLAAD's 20 Under 20 LGBTQ+ people changing the world.

In March 2021, Jamie started her podcast *Lavender You*, providing queer media representation for LGBTQ+ women/femmes, interviewing icons such as costume designer and leader of the Stonewall protests Qween Jean, and musicians Tegan and Sara.

Jamie launched a scholarship in September 2021 to financially support US students fighting for climate justice.

Tired of not seeing queer Latinx representation in

animation, in June 2022 Jamie started Pelea Animation, an independent Latinx animation collective, focusing on stories that center queerness and climate justice.

Her dream job is to write gay Disney princess movies.

"In times of darkness, what has saved people, countries, and movements has been ordinary folks having the courage to speak truth to power. You don't have to get it right on the first try. You don't have to come from a wealthy or privileged background to start a movement. You don't have to have all the knowledge and resources from the get-go. If you have a strong vision, resilience, and a refusal to give in, you can make waves."
—JAMIE MARGOLIN

Born: 2001

Website: thisiszerohour.org

Social media:

@jamie_s_margolin

@Jamie_Margolin

Publications: *Youth to Power*

UNITED STATES

JEROME FOSTER II

Illustrated by
DERICK BROOKS

Jerome first learned about climate change when he was 5, while watching a film with his family.

Hey! Are you guys hearing this?

Shouldn't we be doing something?!

Jerome went to high school at Washington Leadership Academy (WLA), funded through XQ Super Schools.

He took courses in advance technology...

...and found a passion for coding and virtual reality. This gave him an idea of how he could communicate the realities of the climate crisis.

He founded his own company, TAU VR, in ninth grade, where he made virtual experiences of littered oceans and oil rigs to encourage empathy.

Whoa! This is awesome. You can totally put yourself in someone else's shoes.

In summer 2018, he traveled to Iceland with *National Geographic* to see what was happening to the glaciers.

Jerome filmed the glaciers in 360-degree VR, so others could experience them from afar. They were there for 5 hours.

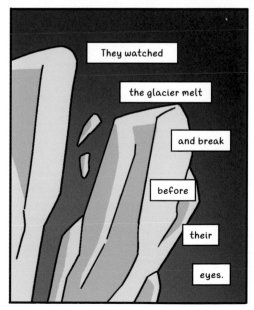

They watched

the glacier melt

and break

before

their

eyes.

We have to do something about this.

Three days later, Jerome was in Washington, DC, at the Youth Climate March he'd helped organize as part of the Zero Hour team. He also began an internship at congressman and civil rights leader John Lewis's office, part of Jerome's dream to one day work in government to take climate action.

Two days later, Zero Hour got an email from Greta Thunberg about her school strike for climate idea.

Jerome was worried at first that striking would conflict with his studies and his internship. But John Lewis and his parents were supportive, and Jerome continued to ask the government to do better.

Jerome testified on behalf of Zero Hour for the Clean Energy DC Act, which at the time was the most aggressive decarbonization bill in history. It passed in 2019.

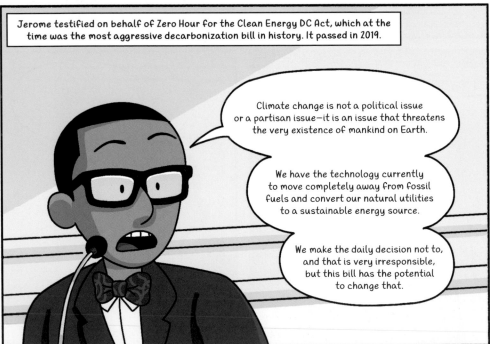

Climate change is not a political issue or a partisan issue—it is an issue that threatens the very existence of mankind on Earth.

We have the technology currently to move completely away from fossil fuels and convert our natural utilities to a sustainable energy source.

We make the daily decision not to, and that is very irresponsible, but this bill has the potential to change that.

In March 2019, Jerome gained international recognition after his passionate speech at Al Gore's Climate Reality Project.

I've seen firsthand how climate change has been decimating our planet. From raging fires to high rising tides to uncontrollable hurricanes. Our planet is begging us to stop.

I feel honored to be here in Atlanta, Georgia, where the civil rights movement began. Civil rights are human rights, and human rights are environmental rights!

Jerome stood outside the White House every Friday for over a year, joining the school strikes for climate.

And in 2021, he was selected to work alongside President Biden as part of the president's Environmental Justice Advisory Council...

...to plan a strategy to combat the climate crisis.

WHAT ARE THEY DOING NOW?

In 2017, at age fifteen, Jerome's virtual reality company, TAU VR, was featured on XQ Super School Live, which aired across major news networks across the US. That year Jerome also founded the Climate Reporter, a news outlet focused on the climate run by international youth.

Jerome is the executive director of OneMillionOfUs, an international youth advocacy and voting rights organization supporting and encouraging young people to create systemic change, which he founded in early 2019.

In late 2019, Jerome helped renowned climate activist and actor Jane Fonda start Fire Drill Fridays, a campaign aimed at older generations to support climate justice in solidarity with the youth.

Jerome was a key organizer for Fridays for Future Washington and protested outside the White House for fifty-eight weeks. He spoke passionately about the Climate Change Education Act, which would make environmental justice a core subject in the US school curriculum.

Jerome studied international environmental policy and advanced calculus at Harvard University in summer 2019 and took part in protests asking Harvard to divest from fossil fuels. In 2020, he went on to study computer science at Pace University.

Jerome is proudly gay and uses his platform to encourage others to be true to themselves: "Joy I believe comes from being genuine to yourself and being real to the world no matter how hard it is at first. Show your pride, spread your joy!"

Jerome is the cofounder of Waic Up, highlighting the stories of marginalized communities and giving them a platform. He has won many awards, including the Captain Planet Foundation's Young Hero for the Earth Award in 2022.

In March 2021, at age eighteen, Jerome became the youngest ever White House adviser, focusing on how to decarbonize the US quickly and equitably, and on improving Black and Indigenous representation in climate policy.

"Us children will rise up and say
'We are the revolution!'
When we demand regulation,
then comes the revelation, and after
the revelation comes the revolution,
and we need a revolution right now."
—JEROME FOSTER II

Born: 2002
Social media:
@jeromefosterii
@JeromeFosterII

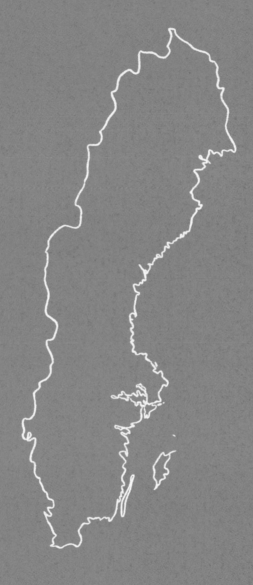

SWEDEN

GRETA THUNBERG

Illustrated by
EMMA REYNOLDS

When Greta learned about the devastating effects of climate change to all life on earth, she was shocked everyone wasn't talking about it every single day. When she was 15, she decided to strike from school every day for 3 weeks outside Swedish parliament, to highlight the climate crisis in the lead-up to the election, as no one in power was talking about this crucial issue.

Greta is autistic, which she says is a superpower and a gift. It allows her to see the climate crisis and the need for urgent action clearly.

She began her strike alone, and not everyone understood.

Why are you doing this?

What is the point of getting an education if politicians won't listen to the top scientists of today?

We won't have a livable future if leaders don't act now.

This is not the way to make a point. You should stay in school and grow up to become someone to make change.

There is simply not enough time for that. This leaflet has all the facts.

More and more people came by and wanted to learn more about the crisis and her strike.

Can we sit with you?

And very soon, more students wanted to join her.

Greta posted a photo of her School Strike for Climate on social media and it quickly went viral. Even more students joined her on strike every day until election night. After the election, Greta and the other students vowed to continue striking from school every Friday outside parliament until Sweden is in line with the Paris Agreement.

Everyone is welcome. Everyone is needed. Please join me. #FridaysForFuture

SAVE OUR SEAS

FRIDAYS FOR FUTURE SOS

PEOPLE NOT PROFIT SYSTEM CHANGE NOT CLIMATE CHANGE!

FRIDAYS FOR FUTURE

Fridays for Future was born, and soon other cities joined them across the world, on every continent.

ACT NOW

DON'T BE A FOSSIL FOOL!

FFF

CLIMATE JUSTICE STRIKE 4 ♥ CLIMATE

THERE IS NO PLANET B!

Greta, you've been invited to speak at COP24 in Poland to represent the young people!

Greta and her dad traveled all over Europe in their electric car, or by public transport, so Greta could speak to many world leaders.

SKOLSTREJK FÖR KLIMATET

For 25 years, countless people have stood in front of the United Nations climate conferences, asking our nations' leaders to stop the emissions. But clearly, this has not worked, as the emissions continue to rise. We have come here to let them know that change is coming, whether you like it or not. You speak of green, eternal economic growth, because you are too scared of being unpopular. You only talk about moving forward with the same bad ideas that got us into this mess. But I don't care about being popular, I care about climate justice and the living planet.

Greta's direct, bold speeches to leaders made headlines worldwide.

January 25, 2019—World Economic Forum, Davos, Switzerland

I am here to say, our house is on fire. Solving the climate crisis is the greatest and most complex challenge that *homo sapiens* have ever faced. The main solution, however, is so simple that even a small child can understand it. We have to stop our emissions of greenhouse gases. And either we do that or we don't. You say that nothing in life is black or white. But that is a lie. A very dangerous lie. Either we prevent a 1.5°C of warming or we don't. Either we avoid setting off that irreversible chain reaction beyond human control—or we don't. Either we choose to go on as a civilization or we don't. That is as black or white as it gets.

There are no gray areas when it comes to survival. Now we all have a choice. We can create transformational action that will safeguard the living conditions for future generations. Or we can continue with business as usual and fail.

We must change almost everything in our current societies. The bigger your carbon footprint, the bigger your duty. The bigger your platform, the bigger your responsibility.

I don't want you to be hopeful. I want you to panic. I want you to feel the fear I feel every day. And then I want you to act. I want you to act as you would in a crisis. I want you to act as if your house is on fire. Because it is.

On March 15, 2019, the first Global Climate Strike took place, with over 1 million people at 2,200 events in 125 countries.

A few months later, on May 24, hundreds of thousands of school students went on strike for the second Global Climate Strike.

In September 2019, Greta and her dad sailed across the Atlantic Ocean on a zero-carbon racing boat with a small crew.

It took them over two weeks, and was a very hard journey, but not flying was vital to Greta because of the huge emissions from air travel.

Greta missed her two dogs, her mum, and her sister back home very much.

Hundreds of supporters came to greet them at the port in New York.

September 23, 2019—
UN General Assembly, New York City, USA

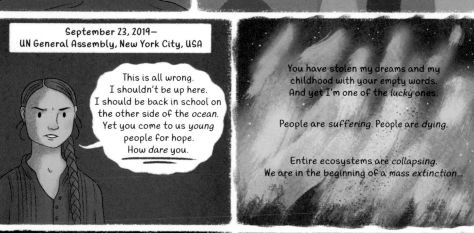

This is all wrong. I shouldn't be up here. I should be back in school on the other side of the *ocean*. Yet you come to us *young* people for hope. How *dare* you.

You have stolen my dreams and my childhood with your empty words. And yet I'm one of the *lucky* ones.

People are *suffering*. People are *dying*.

Entire ecosystems are *collapsing*. We are in the beginning of a mass *extinction*...

...and all you can talk about is *money* and fairy tales of eternal economic growth. How *dare* you.

You are failing us. But the young people are starting to understand your betrayal. The eyes of all future generations are upon you. And if you choose to fail us, I say: we will *never* forgive you.

We will not let you get away with this. Right here, right now is where we draw the line.

Last week, well over 4 million people in over 170 countries striked for the climate. We marched for a living planet and a safe future for everyone. We spoke the science, and demanded that the people in power would listen to and act on the science. But our political leaders didn't listen. So today we are millions around the world striking and marching again. And we will keep doing it until they listen.

And we promise: once they start taking the responsibility and do their job, we will stop worrying and go back to school, go back to work.

We are not communicating our opinions or political views. The climate and ecological crisis is beyond party politics. We are communicating the current best available science.

We are not in school today. You are not at work today. Because this is an *emergency*. And we will not be bystanders. Some would say we are wasting lesson time; we say we are changing the world. So that when we are older, we will be able to look our children in the eyes and say that we did everything we could back then.

We have been told so many times that there's no point in doing this, that we won't have an impact anyway. I think we have proven that to be wrong by now. Through history, the most important changes in society have come from the bottom up, from grassroots.

We are the change, and change is coming.

During Global Week for Future, between September 20-27, 2019, over 7.6 million people from over 185 countries came together in the largest global climate protests in human history.

Fridays for Future and "the Greta effect" brought global attention to the climate crisis, inspiring millions of people to unite and take action to change the world.

WHAT ARE THEY DOING NOW?

Greta talks openly about the gift of being autistic, which has encouraged and inspired many other autistic people around the world. She has written several books and been featured in international press, books, and documentaries. Greta has won many prestigious awards, including the International Children's Peace Prize, the Rachel Carson Award, and the Ambassador of Conscience Award for Fridays for Future—Amnesty International's highest honor.

Greta was inspired by the March for Our Lives and Zero Hour student-led protests in the US when starting her activism and spurred on by the heat waves in Sweden. Growing up, Greta struggled with OCD compulsions and her mental health. She was anxious in groups, so began by protesting alone. Greta's health and well-being dramatically improved once she began her activism, as she had found a sense of purpose and like-minded people.

From August 2019-August 2020, Greta took a yearlong sabbatical from school so she could focus on her activism and travel to speak to world leaders.

When the COVID-19 pandemic was announced, she encouraged people to strike online to stay safe with #ClimateStrikeOnline and post a photo of their sign.

Greta said in a BBC interview that she's very stubborn and "if I'm committed to something I go all in" but that she doesn't like all the attention that comes with it. "If I were to choose I would just be like everyone else and continue studying because that's what I enjoy doing the most. But since this is such an extraordinary situation, we have to do things that we might not always find very comfortable."

Greta quickly became one of the most famous and influential youth climate activists and continues to inspire people around the world with her activism. "The Greta effect" galvanized millions of people into action, and she continues to strike every Friday.

"The people in power don't need conferences, treaties, or agreements to start taking real climate action. They can start today. When enough people come together, then change will come and we can achieve almost anything. So instead of looking for hope—start creating it."
—GRETA THUNBERG

Born: 2003
Website: fridaysforfuture.org
Social media:
⬜ @gretathunberg
🐦 @GretaThunberg
Publications: *The Climate Book*; *No One Is Too Small to Make a Difference*; *I Know This to Be True: Greta Thunberg: On Truth, Courage, and Saving Our Planet*; *Our House Is on Fire: Scenes of a Family and a Planet in Crisis.*

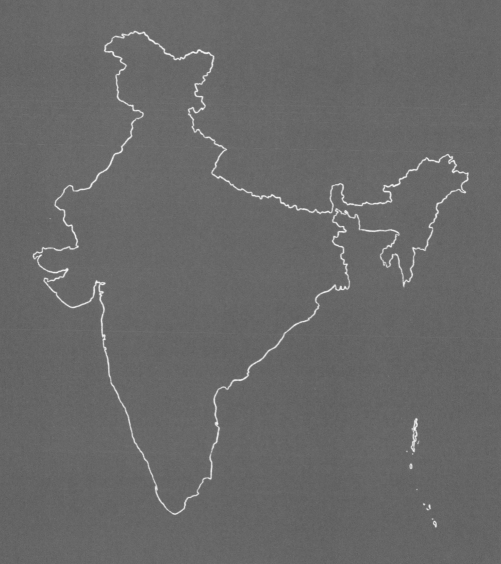

INDIA

RIDHIMA PANDEY

Illustrated by
SHIVANA SOOKDEO

Ridhima was born in Nainital, in the Himalayan mountains. Her parents are wildlife conservationists, and Ridhima has always loved animals.

When she was 5, they moved to Haridwar, an important holy city for Hindus. The sacred River Ganges runs through here, where people bathe and many religious ceremonies are held.

But then, something terrible happened.

Oh no... Dinesh! Come quickly!

Mummy?

Mummy? Daddy? What is it?

Reporting here live...

Mummy, why did this happen?

Well...climate change causes more extreme weather events, like this flood. Your dad and I work hard with other scientists to learn about this, and to get governments to listen, to try and heal the earth, to stop things like this from happening.

...the state of Uttarakhand has been completely devastated by this flash flood... Scientists are saying this is the country's worst natural disaster since the tsunami in 2004...

Thousands of people died. Ridhima was haunted by what she had seen, and wished she could do something.

I want to help too!

That was the moment Ridhima decided to become a climate activist.

When Ridhima was 9, she filed a lawsuit petition against the Indian government for failing to take significant action against climate change, stating they had broken their promise made in the Paris Agreement.

She said they needed to regulate greenhouse gas emissions and reduce fossil fuels, since India was one of the most vulnerable countries to climate change and already experiencing the effects.

But Ridhima did not lose hope! And soon her story reached media around the globe.

Disappointingly, the National Green Tribunal dismissed her petition.

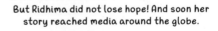

My government has failed to take steps to reduce greenhouse gas emissions, which are causing extreme climate conditions.

This will impact both me and future generations.

Even though the Ganges is a holy river, and many religious ceremonies take place upon it, people still pollute the water with garbage and human sewage. Ridhima has tried many times to speak to people littering and the authorities about it, but has been ignored.

Please do not throw your garbage here!

Ridhima joined young activists around the world in the climate strikes, but she found they were not taken seriously in India. So she started focusing on educating and empowering kids her age who were eager to help.

In September 2019, she traveled to New York to speak at the United Nations when she was just 11.

I'm so proud of you, Ridhima.

Thanks, Dad!

As part of Global Climate Week, Ridhima and 15 other children from all over the world filed an official complaint to the United Nations Committee on the Rights of the Child. They accused 5 of the world's biggest carbon-polluting countries (Argentina, Brazil, Germany, France, and Turkey) of violating the Convention on the Rights of the Child, saying that they failed to take action on the climate crisis and stop supporting the use of fossil fuels.

I want to save the future of all the children and all people of future generations.

In late 2019, Ridhima was attending an event in Delhi when the whole city became engulfed in thick smoke pollution blown over from farmers burning millions of tons of crop waste. Although it's illegal to burn the rice fields in order to quickly prepare the same fields for the wheat crop, farmers feel they have no alternative. A public health crisis was announced, and children were kept in their houses to keep them from the fumes.

This has been happening every year for decades, and Delhi is already one of the worst polluted cities in the world. Ridhima wrote to the prime minister with an online petition called "Basho Ke Maan Ki Baat" (Talk about the value of children), but she never got a reply.

And for a while in India, the skies were blue again.

Although the lockdowns were only temporary, it shows that the world could come together in an emergency, just like we need to for the climate crisis.

In spring 2020, many factories and traffic across the world stopped emitting pollution because of the COVID-19 global pandemic.

Ridhima has given many TEDx Talks and inspiring speeches at international conferences and events.

The children of today and the children of the future will be bearing the brunt and the effects of what is happening now... It pains me to my very core that children that are not part of this decision-making process have to suffer. I can't leave the safety of my future in someone else's hands who doesn't care about it. If I, a 12-year-old child, can understand how detrimental the effects of climate change are and can raise my voice against it, all of you in the audience can only do better. Let's start acting now, and let's save our planet together, because it's *our* planet.

When she is not studying at school, Ridhima travels around her country and gives talks to the public. She continues to inspire, educate, and empower others.

WHAT ARE THEY DOING NOW?

In September 2020, on the very first International Day of Clean Air for Blue Skies, Ridhima wrote an open letter to the prime minister of India, Narendra Modi, demanding clean, safe air, or all citizens would end up living her worst nightmare and carrying oxygen cylinders so they could breathe.

In October 2021, the UN Committee on the Rights of the Child refused to hear the #ChildrenVsClimateCrisis case and dismissed it. So the next month, #ChildrenVsClimateCrisis submitted a petition to the UN secretary general, urging him to declare the climate crisis a global emergency. They continue to fight, and you can see the latest developments at childrenvsclimatecrisis.org.

Ridhima planned several Fridays for Future Haridwar Global Strikes, and in summer 2021 she started her own organization called Environment Conservation Trust. She was part of EarthDay.org's "My Future My Voice," a collection of messages from fifty inspiring youth activists from seventeen countries, and has worked with UNICEF. Ridhima spoke at YOUTHTOPIA Younite 2021, and in November 2021 she was a member of the Civil Society & Youth Advisory council for COP26.

Ridhima's awards and honors include: being listed as one of BBC's top 100 most inspiring, influential women in 2020, winning the Sanctuary Nature Foundation Young Naturalist Award in 2020, and winning the Mother Teresa Memorial Award for Social Justice in 2021. Global Landscapes Forum named Ridhima as one of "16 Women Restoring the Earth 2022," and she won the MRFA Foundation and ISCAR Women Changemaker of the Year and Brand Ambassador award in 2022.

"Mother Nature does not need us,
we need her, and we all have to
understand that as soon as we can.
We humans have created this ideology
that humans are superior [to] other species
but this is not true, we cannot survive
without them and everyone living on
this planet is important for
each other to survive."
—RIDHIMA PANDEY

Born: 2009
Social media:
🔲 @ridhimapandeyy
🐦 @ridhimapandey7

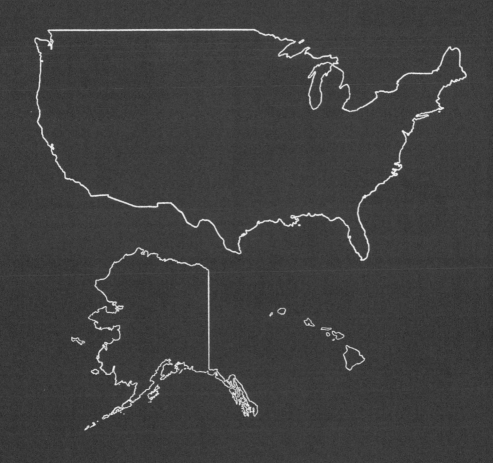

UNITED STATES

DAPHNE FRIAS

Illustrated by
DEVON HOLZWARTH

In 2016, Daphne went to college at SUNY Oswego in upstate New York.

The college campus is right next to Lake Ontario, a beautiful place where students hang out to relax between classes.

But the tides have been rising every year, causing erosion every summer along the shoreline, destroying houses by the lake. There was even flooding in Daphne's student dorms.

Oh boy...

This is messed up.

Daphne also noticed that even though the lake was important to the students, they didn't look after it. Single-use plastic from her college littered the lake *everywhere*.

This makes literally no sense... Why isn't anyone else angry about this?

Daphne met up with her friends.

Did you guys notice that there's a ton of garbage by the lake? Hanging out by Lake Ontario is a rite of passage for students here but it's a total dump— make it make sense!

Yeah, I know!

It's so bad, but it always happens.

Well, we're gonna do something about it!

Daphne knew the first step was bringing back respect to the lake and stopping littering from single-use plastic. They worked hard with the college's sustainability club to budget for paper alternatives.

Campus administration to:
-Eliminate 324,000 single-use plastic cups from the dining halls each semester.
-Reduce their carbon footprint by terminating manufacture and sale of single-use school-branded plastic water bottles.
-Increase voting seats of the office of sustainability on committees that make decisions affecting the campus environment.
-Request for greater sustainability education with new incoming freshmen.

They presented this at the student government assembly.

It took a lot of hard work to hold their college accountable to enact the changes, but in May 2019 their amendment passed!

Woooo, we did it!

It's *super* important to remember that the systems that led us to the climate crisis and to gun violence are the *exact same systems*. Because the same communities that are disproportionately affected by one are disproportionately affected by the other.

In February 2018, after the devastating Parkland school shooting, students led a demonstration called March for Our Lives (MFOL). Growing up in Harlem with a high level of gun violence, Daphne knew she had to do something. The nearest march from Harlem was hours away with no good transport links, so Daphne worked diligently to organize two buses to transport over 100 students from Harlem so they could join the march. In August 2019, she was appointed as New York state director for MFOL for a year.

On September 20, 2019, during the Global Week for Climate Action, Daphne was an official spokesperson and was able to speak up for her community on a large scale.

She gave speeches to thousands of people from all backgrounds, including other disabled youth climate activists. Daphne has gone on to speak at many climate rallies, highlighting how the climate crisis disproportionally affects the disabled community.

I want people to know that, similarly to our Indigenous siblings, our Black and brown siblings: people with disabilities have been fighting against the climate crisis for *so long*. We have experienced this firsthand for *so long*. Things like air quality for people with respiratory illnesses—if the air quality is decreasing, so is our ability to be able to breathe.

If there is a natural disaster, or a snowstorm and power outage, I need to be able to charge my wheelchair. I wouldn't be able to just get up and evacuate. As snowstorms become even more unpredictable, there have been numerous times where I haven't been able to leave my house.

DAPHNE FRIAS

Up to about age 7 or 8 I was ambulatory and I used to walk...

Growing up, I realized that I'd tied my success to my ability to be able to walk, because that's what society told me I needed to do in order to be successful. It took so *much* of dismantling that harmful rhetoric in my brain for me to realize: I can be just as badass rolling around doing my thing, and I don't need to be standing on two feet to be able to do that.

71

WHAT ARE THEY DOING NOW?

Alongside her climate activism, in 2018, before the US midterm election, Daphne started a nonprofit called Box the Ballot, to make sure votes from disenfranchised communities and absentee ballots were counted. Thanks to Daphne and students in over seventy college chapters, they were able to send nearly 470,000 absentee ballots to be counted in the 2018 midterms.

As part of the Sustainable Development Goal 16 at the UN Major Group for Children and Youth, in spring 2019, Daphne was appointed as one of the North American Regional Focal Points, where her role is to highlight youth activist voices and their work as pivotal peacemakers.

In June 2019, Daphne won her election as County Committee Representative of Assembly District 70, Election District 80, in West Harlem, where she continues to work hard for her community.

Daphne's work and her story have been featured in high-profile books, magazines, and newspapers around the world. Her honors include the Premios Juventud Agent of Change Award 2021, NowThis Next honoree in the Disability Rights Category 2021, and Univision Angel of Channel 41 for July 2021. At COP26 in 2021, Daphne was part of a panel at the *New York Times* Climate Hub, moderated by Emma Watson.

Daphne continues to be a passionate changemaker as a freelance organizer, speaking at colleges, panels, and summits, and consulting with nonprofits to create engaging campaigns to amplify the voice of Gen Z.

"Just because you have
a disability, doesn't mean the
world isn't your oyster.
You are entirely powerful
in the whole entire way that
your body is made."
—DAPHNE FRIAS

Born: 1998
Website: daphnefrias.com
Social media:
📷 @frias_daphne
🐦 @frias_daphne

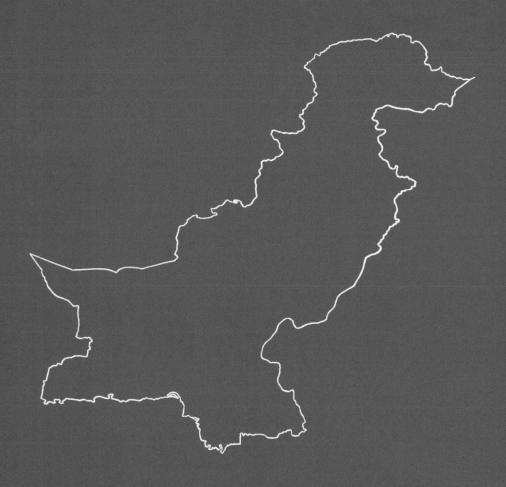

PAKISTAN

IQBAL BADRUDDIN JAMAL

Illustrated by
ANOOSHA SYED

Iqbal started by telling his friend Kamran about it.

Pakistan is only responsible for 1% of global emissions, but it's one of the most vulnerable countries to the effects of climate change.

So I asked myself, what *can* be done as individuals to stop this?

Soon, more friends joined them, and they met up every week to discuss this issue and what they could do about it.

They started to speak to their local community about climate change.

Most didn't want to hear what they had to say. As citizens of a developing country, people were focused on income and survival.

Others follow religious teachings, and many said the floods were simply acts of God.

For the next 8 years, Pakistan, like much of the world, was not ready to hear about climate change.

Iqbal and his friends did not give up, and they continued to meet and pick up litter in nature whenever they could.
Kamran Ali - Ameera Adil - Iqbal Badruddin Jamal - Yaser Hameed - Rozina Ahmed

In late 2018, they saw young European activists like Greta Thunberg striking from school, even though their countries were not yet as affected by climate change. Iqbal was heartened by this.

Iqbal started Fridays for Future Pakistan and they began to strike every week, outside the dean's office or main hall.

Iqbal and his friends traveled to speak at 35 universities over 3 months to spread their message. They spoke to students all over Pakistan, and more teenagers and adults joined them.

In Islamabad at the Global Climate Strike on September 20, 2019, over 4,000 people joined them. Reporters were shocked; they had never seen a protest like this in the capital before.

CLIMATE JUSTICE!

MARCH NOW OR SWIM LATER

ISLAMABAD CLIMATE MARCH

CLIM CHAN NO

As more people became aware of the climate crisis, speaking with communities became easier. In rural areas, the team explained how climate change would affect their farming and crops due to extreme weather changes.

When speaking in urban areas, they focused on how climate change affects the economy. The team also spoke to influential clerics, encouraging them to share awareness in their daily teachings on TV.

Climate change is now common knowledge in Pakistan—thanks to Iqbal and his friends.

The government launched national campaigns and has planted billions of trees. Iqbal and his team continue to travel around Pakistan to pass on their knowledge about climate change and appreciating nature. And at last, people are happy to listen.

WHAT ARE THEY DOING NOW?

After getting his degree in international relations from Iqra University in 2016, Iqbal worked for environmental organization WaterAid Pakistan as a research associate, and as a climate change officer at LEAD Pakistan to inspire future leaders. In 2017 he dedicated himself to his activism and awareness campaigns full-time. In 2022, Iqbal became the Stone Soup Leadership Institute's Global Education Outreach Coordinator. Iqbal has a master's in climate change, and in the future hopes to create a platform to share knowledge between the West and Global South.

Iqbal is passionate about empowering local communities to develop their own sustainable future and is asking the government to introduce climate education in Pakistan.

Pakistan is the eigth most vulnerable nation to climate change in the world despite being one of the lowest emitters, and is already experiencing severe climate emergencies such as the devastating floods in 2022. Temperatures are soaring into uninhabitable levels earlier every year, affecting water and electricity access and destroying crops. Pakistan's seaport Gwadar collects the untreated water from the two biggest global polluters—India and China—and this harmful polluted water then flows into the rivers and seas. People in Pakistan suffering from poverty, war, and lack of access to quality education are especially vulnerable to climate change. Iqbal, Fridays for Future Pakistan, and Pakistan's government are urging international leaders to act now.

"COVID taught us that we can live without luxury. People can grow their own things, and live a very simple life, and give back to nature. COVID also told the world, if we can take this action as an emergency, we can also take this action for the climate."

—IQBAL BADRUDDIN JAMAL

Born: 1992
Social media:
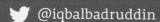 @iqbalbadruddin

AUSTRALIA

JEAN HINCHLIFFE

Illustrated by
ERIN HUNTING

The Project
Nov. 30, 2018

Massive turnout today! How does it make you feel?

So ecstatic! The strike was amazing!

I see climate change as such an important issue, as do most young people. Because I see politicians doing *nothing* I feel like I *need* to take action and I *need* to help make change.

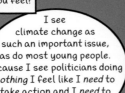

On December 8, 2018, youth and adults marched together to protest the Adani coal mine, a controversial and environmentally disastrous fossil fuel project.

We need to stop Adani! It's going to be pushing Australia and the rest of the world back from a sustainable future.

SAY **NO** TO COAL!

ADANI GO HOME!!

#STOP ADANI

#SchoolStrike4Climate kept growing, with 150,000 people across Australia striking at the first Global Climate Strike in March 2019, and over 300,000 at the September 2019 Global Climate Strikes, joining more than 7 million people worldwide in the biggest climate protest event in history to date.

Being at these protests and seeing young people and adults all coming together gives me hope!

It's not just gonna be one protest that will totally change the world, but it's these movements, everyone working together, that creates this tipping point where politicians *have* to do something. I would love to see our government treat the climate crisis as the crisis that it *is*.

ANIMALS MATTER + ♡

STOP CLIMATE CRIME

Jean's TEDx Talk, May 2019

As we demanded immediate action from our politicians, we created a totally unprecedented demonstration of *youth power*. The younger a person is, the more they will be impacted by climate change, and the less voice they're given today. However, when young people are given a voice, we can *completely* change the conversation.

Gen Z, our generation, are the first to grow up with the internet at our disposal. Without Google, my knowledge of the climate crisis and its impacts upon the world would be significantly smaller. We have an innate understanding of how social media functions, and how to create content other kids will engage with. This translated to the strike growing massively in size as soon as we began spreading our message online.

In movements that aren't led by adults, but instead by passionate teenagers, there is total *freedom*. We decide on the goals, the image we want for ourselves. Together, we really do thrive.
While we can't vote, we've been able to make more change than we ever thought possible.

In 2021, Jean's first book came out, in which she shares her knowledge of youth activism and how to make systemic change.

WHAT ARE THEY DOING NOW?

From June 2019–May 2020, Australia experienced a bushfire megafire and a state of emergency was declared. Spring 2020 was also when Jean and her school strike peers took their action to social media during COVID-19 lockdowns.

Jean has regularly been featured in international press, including *The Project*, *Foreign Correspondent*, and *The Feed*. In May 2019, Jean was awarded the Amy Large Young Volunteer of the Year Award.

Alongside her activism, Jean is an actress. Her roles include Gemma in the series *The Unlisted* and Pia in *Les Norton*.

In a landmark world first, in May 2021 students succeeded in getting the Australian federal court to order their environment minister to protect children from the harmful impacts of a proposed coal mine expansion. One of students involved, Ava Princi, said, "We understand it is the first time a court of law, anywhere in the world, has ordered a government to specifically protect young people from the catastrophic harms of climate change." A step in the right direction.

Aboriginal and Torres Strait Islander Peoples are especially vulnerable to climate change. Jean says in a 9Honey interview: "Listening to Indigenous communities and their philosophies is crucial. These communities are bearing most of the brunt in Australia and have been at the forefront of knowing how to exist with the earth, rather than taking from it."

Climate change remains a major political issue in Australia, as one of the world's biggest carbon emitters and producers of coal and gas. Jean and #SchoolStrike4Climate, Indigenous peoples, university students, trade unions, and allies continue to protest for climate justice.

"Our politicians refuse to listen to the educated, so why should we be sitting in history class when we could be on the streets making history itself?"
—JEAN HINCHLIFFE

Born: 2004
Website: schoolstrike4climate.com
Social media:
@jeanlola.h
@jean_hinchliffe
Publications: *Lead the Way*

RUSSIA

ARSHAK MAKICHYAN

Illustrated by
MARGARITA KUKHTINA

ARSHAK MAKICHYAN
Moscow, Russia

Winter 2018

GREENPEACE
International

Have you seen this about Greta Thunberg?... I know, it's crazy we've learned about the climate crisis from a girl in Sweden, not from school...

I read Russia is the fourth-highest emitter of greenhouse gases, but no one is talking about this...

Yeah... Well, activism isn't a part of Russian culture... I know, we'd be arrested if we gathered in a group like in Europe...

Yeah, I know... Sometimes it feels like we're living on another planet.

It's different here.

In February 2019, Arshak went to his first ever protest, a march in memory of liberal politician Boris Nemtsov, who was assassinated in 2015. Permits for protests are incredibly difficult to get approved, but it gave Arshak some hope.

In March, Arshak went to a protest as part of the Global Climate Strike. Hyde Park in Moscow is the only place the government allows people to protest in a large group, but this park is deliberately far away from the busy crowds of people in the city center, so protests here go mostly unnoticed.

About 70 people went, and the media largely ignored it out of fear of the government if they reported it.

Group protests are almost impossible to get permission for, but solo protests are allowed. So Arshak decided to protest alone in Pushkin Square, where it is always busy.

Solidarity!

ЗАБАСТОВКА ЗА КЛИМАТ

A lot of people were supportive.

Some were not.

ЗАБАСТОВКА ЗА КЛИМАТ

We're photographing your passport.

Frustrated at the government for continually refusing his requests for peaceful group strikes, and those under 18 not being allowed to strike at all, Arshak organized an online flash mob on Twitter and received support from all around the world.

FOR CLIMATE

#LET RUSSIA STRIKE FOR CLIMAT

LET RUSSIA STRIKE FOR CLIMATE

LET RU STRI FOR CLIMA

LET RUSSIA STRIKE FOR CLIMATE

LET RI STRIKE CLIM

Arshak Makichyan

We will continue our flash mob until everyone has the right to fight for climate and the future.
#LetRussiaStrike ForClimate

A lot of people in Russia still didn't believe in, or understand, climate change, but in summer 2019, the worst floods in their history struck Irkutsk, and forest fires spread through Siberia. These catastrophes convinced people that something was seriously wrong. More activists joined Arshak, and they founded Fridays for Future Russia.

My 5 minutes is up, your turn!

Thanks, Arshak!

ЗА КЛИМАТ

GLOBAL STRIKE FOR CLIMATE

When their mass protest requests were denied for the September 20 Global Climate Strike, they formed a queue and took turns to hold up their signs, so it still counted as a solo protest.

Over 700 people in over 35 cities in Russia took part. A few days later, there was a big victory for the protestors: the government finally ratified the Paris Agreement, 4 years after joining.

After they were refused permission to peacefully protest as a group over 10 times, Arshak and 2 others held a protest anyway, despite knowing what the consequences would be, as they believed it was their right.

They were all detained after the protest, with Arshak awaiting trial and the other two being fined. Arshak was invited to speak at COP25 in Madrid, and went knowing that he would be arrested on his return.

December 2019, Madrid

I am from Russia, where everyone can be arrested for anything, but I am not afraid to be arrested. I am afraid not to do enough. And I think, and I believe, that we can change everything, because behind us there are millions of people, behind us there is science, and activism is a solution. So please, act now.

 **Greta Thunberg**

December 22, 2019
This is Arshak Makichyan. He has been sentenced to 6 days in detention for peacefully standing up for everyone's future. Support him and his fellow co-strikers — join the #ClimateStrike

 **Annika Kruse**

December 21, 2019
It's horrifying to me how some countries still not only ignore scientific facts, but also basic human rights.

As expected, when Arshak returned, he was arrested as an organizer and jailed for 6 days.

All around the world, activists and climate groups shared messages of support with #FreeArshak and protested outside their Russian embassies over his unfairly severe punishment.

Arshak continues to fight for the climate and against Putin's war, and for the freedom and human right to peacefully protest.

In October 2022, in a terrifying decision by the government, Arshak and the other men in his family were stripped of their Russian citizenship and were all made stateless.

WHAT ARE THEY DOING NOW?

In June 2021, Arshak denounced his activism so he could run for Russian parliament. Unfortunately, the party that promised to nominate him got threats from security services. So he continued with his activism and protested alongside other youth activists at COP26.

In January 2022, Arshak's partner and fellow activist, Polina Oleinikova, was detained and fined for posting anti-police-torture posters. The next day, the police arrived at her home. She managed to avoid arrest and escape the building dressed as a man in Arshak's clothes. They decided that night to get married so they would have the right to visit each other if either was imprisoned. A month later, on their wedding day, Putin declared war on Ukraine. They said their vows and protested with their clothing: an anti-war slogan on Arshak's shirt, Polina in a bright blue dress holding yellow flowers like the Ukrainian flag.

They originally planned to stay in Russia, but feared for their safety after several arrests. So they fled to Berlin in Germany, where they could freely protest the war and lobby EU politicians to ban fossil fuels—the main source of funding for Putin's war.

Arshak is originally from Armenia, and has been a Russian citizen for most of his life. To punish Arshak for his ongoing activism, the Russian government stripped Arshak, his two brothers, and his father of their Russian citizenship.

Arshak hopes in the future he can help other activists from totalitarian regimes be heard.

"In a country where there have been no elections for twenty years, every day is an election. We choose every day to be activists and oppose this terrible system."

"When I started my activism, I had no support in Russia. It was great to get support from other countries. International solidarity is very important for fighting global crises. And it was great to find a lot of new friends all around the world."

—ARSHAK MAKICHYAN

Born: 1994
Social media:
 @makichyan.arshak
 @MakichyanA

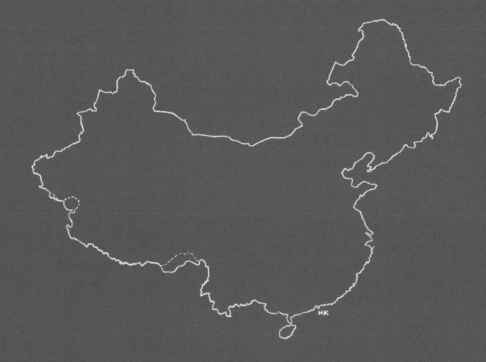

CHINA

ŌU HÓNGYÌ
欧 泓 奕
AKA
HOWEY OU

Illustrated by
JADE ZHANG

Then,

she had a dream...

Ōu Hóngyì and her family were in a restaurant where they had to catch and kill the fish in their buckets, or they would not eat.

She couldn't grab the fish.

Their eyes met...

...and the fish...

EXPLODED

She woke up with her heart racing.

I will never harm a living creature again.

Ōu Hóngyì committed to a vegan diet, and eventually, her parents became vegetarian too.

Later in 2018, she heard about Greta Thunberg and the school strikes. She spent hours researching.

There is not one single school striker in Mainland China? But our country has the highest carbon emissions...

Ōu Hóngyǐ used a VPN—a virtual private network—giving her access to more websites. She reached out to other activists and joined Twitter.

In that case, I will be the first to do something.

She began day one of her strikes outside the Guilin government buildings.

HOWEY OU
#FRIDAYSFORFUTURE

GRETA THUNBERG
May 26, 2019
Howey Ou is a true hero. We are all behind you. Guilin, China.
#FridaysForFuture

ANNA TAYLOR
May 27, 2019
This is perhaps the bravest thing I have seen so far in the #FridaysForFuture movement. Please follow Howey Ou and show your support ♥

气候危机
学校罢保
CLIMATE CRISIS
SCHOOL STRIKE

DRUE SLATTER
May 28, 2019
Last week saw the second global #ClimateStrike by 1.6 million students worldwide. Not all of us come from places with the privilege of striking. This girl held the only climate strike that happened in Mainland China. On her own, 21km from her home. Brave.

Ōu Hóngyǐ's picture quickly went viral and she received international support.

After 7 days, she was arrested and questioned by the authorities and told not to speak to foreign journalists or tweet about it.

Ōu Hóngyǐ, are you all right?! They kept phoning us at work about you.

And they've cut off our internet at home...

And your school...

They've barred you from going unless you stop this... We're worried about you.

After Ōu Hóngyì's story went viral, her school agreed she could continue her studies if she gave up her activism. Ōu Hóngyì continued to strike every Friday.

Every Friday morning she spent her allowance on tree saplings from the local market and planted them with her friends.

She called the initiative #PlantForSurvival.

Ōu Hóngyì,

we know this is important to you, but you have to focus on your studies too...

I have to keep going. This is the most important thing.

Her parents and school were under a lot of pressure from the authorities, so she decided to move out to live in a hostel in the city.

In 2019, 16-year-old Ōu Hóngyì set out on a solo tour of the country for several months, to raise awareness of the climate crisis.

We plant trees every Friday, on the banks and in communities around us, until our nation, our government, is in line with the Paris Agreement.

We are rising; we are unstoppable.

She has reached millions of people, and has supporters worldwide.

Her bravery encouraged many others to join her and speak up for the climate.

WHAT ARE THEY DOING NOW?

In May 2020, Ōu Hóngyì celebrated the one-year anniversary of China's climate strike movement with eleven other activists from six cities, each posting their pictures and drawings online. Since then, many have been forced to stop being activists after pressure from the government and police.

Ōu Hóngyì regularly screened climate films in coffee shops on Saturdays, and she toured to major Chinese cities to screen the Greta Thunberg documentary.

In July 2020, when China experienced the worst flooding in decades, Ōu Hóngyì started the hashtag #ChinaFloods, stressing that they were caused by the climate crisis.

In September 2020, she organized a silent protest with three other activists in front of the Shanghai Exhibition Center and was detained. Greta Thunberg tweeted her support and criticized China's poor treatment of activists.

Ōu Hóngyì left China in late January 2021 to study in Berlin for six months and travel Europe to connect with fellow activists. She vowed to strike for climate wherever she goes.

After protesting against the expansion of the Lafarge-Holcim limestone quarry in Lausanne, Switzerland, Ōu Hóngyì was fined and sentenced to sixty days in prison. She began a hunger strike on April 19, 2021, in protest.

In November 2021 at COP26 in Glasgow, Ōu Hóngyì spoke on a panel about better educating and engaging students. She said it's important to consider the nuance when discussing China's failure on climate: "The developed countries shifted the basic manufacturing industries to the Global South to use their land, water, and air to avoid the pollution, while the local nature and human lives there are being exploited."

Meeting activists from all over the world has encouraged her to keep fighting. Ōu Hóngyì's actions—especially against the adversity she's faced—has encouraged others to speak out and hold their country accountable to their climate promises.

"I think we all have a connection to nature in our hearts. We all have a love for nature, and a respect for it. But a lot of people are disconnected from nature because of industrialization and modernization . . . So we are out of touch with nature, we forget that we are connected to nature."

"Meditating alone in nature really helps to remind you to share the love and gratitude you have for Earth with everyone you meet and with every word you speak."
—ŌU HÓNGYÌ

Born: 2002
[Instagram] @howey_ou
[Twitter] @howey_ou

UGANDA

LEAH NAMUGERWA

Illustrated by
NATASHA NAYO

Fourteen-year-old Leah began her Friday School Strike on February 8, 2019, after she saw children her age on TV starving, losing their homes and their lives because of extreme weather events caused by climate change.

Inspired by Greta Thunberg, she wanted to start a campaign in her home country, Uganda.

FRIDAYS FOR FUTURE

Many months without rain causes droughts, and crops cannot grow, meaning many people go hungry.

Deforestation (trees cut down for fuel) is so extreme in Uganda that it has caused desertification, meaning previously fertile areas of land can no longer support plant growth.

Unpredictable rainstorms cause dangerous flooding and mudslides, made worse by the lack of trees. These deadly events displace and claim the lives of thousands of Ugandans every year.

Uganda has one of the youngest populations in the world, with a median age of 16. East Africans will be some of the worst affected by climate change, with many already enduring the effects.

Along with her cousin Bob Matovu, Hilda Flavia Nakabuye, and Nirere Sadrach, Leah formed Fridays for Future Uganda, and soon many other young people joined them in weekly and global climate strikes.

School Strike for Climate!

FRIDAYS FOR FUTURE UGANDA

They faced many challenges, including police intimidation and parents forbidding their children from missing school to join them.

Tsk! Ignore them.

I know I'm doing the right thing.

You're standing up for your future! So keep going, Leah.

As long as it makes you happy, then I'm happy too.

We're proud of you!

But her mom, dad, and uncle have always supported her. Her uncle is an environmentalist who runs Green Campaign Africa and offers his informal support to FFF Uganda.

Leah joined social media and soon connected with fellow activists and thousands of followers all around the world. In May 2019 she began her campaign and petition to ban plastic in Uganda.

🏠 Home
\# Explore
🔔 Notifications
✉ Messages
🔖 Bookmarks
🗐 Lists

Fellow activists!

Support my petition using #BanPlasticUG

LEAH NAMUGERWA

0:08 1K views

Trends for you

//////··/////
1,713 Tweets

//··//·
3150 Tweets

//··/////
7527 Tweets

/////·//

110

On September 16, 2019, Greta Thunberg and Fridays for Future activists, including FFF Uganda, were awarded Amnesty International's Ambassador of Conscience Award, their highest human rights honor.

Leah has a huge social media presence and often posts videos to educate people around the world about the harsh realities of Uganda and how the climate crisis is already affecting them.

I have a message from my generation. It's in pain. We're facing a crisis we never created. Children are dying due to extreme weather events.

Last week 10 children died due to mudslides, erratic rainfalls, and floods. All leaders do is talk, talk, talk...I need climate justice for my generation.

Stop talking and act now.

In 2020 and 2021, Leah responded to the Ugandan hunger crisis during the COVID-19 lockdown by starting a youth-led emergency fund, raising over $15,000, which fed over 3,000 children.

My goal is to plant 1 billion trees, but we can only achieve this if we work together.

WHAT ARE THEY DOING NOW?

Leah continues to strike every Friday and is a key member of Fridays for Future Uganda, organizing global climate strikes. She often faces resistance, threat of arrest, and racism when she strikes.

She continues to plant birthday trees with support from her family and the wider community. People all over the world have reached out to Leah to support her mission and plant trees on their birthdays. Much of the public land in Uganda is not suitable for seedlings, and Leah has had great success in planting on privately owned land once the landowners find out about her campaign and want to help.

Leah and other young activists meet to collect garbage and plastic waste from the shore around Lake Victoria near where she went to school, which encourages the locals to keep the area cleaner.

Leah has given many speeches and interviews in Uganda, around the world, and online, including for UN-Habitat, World Urban Forum, ECOSOC Youth Forum, and Earth Uprising Global Youth Summit, and was a youth delegate at COP25.

Leah's future ambitions include going to university to study for a bachelor's degree in environmental science.

"Young people have shown the world that we can get things done— at times better than adults. That's why organizations should have youth representatives on their governing bodies, that's why young people should be involved in climate negotiations. We understand the needs of young people. We have the biggest stake in the future."

—LEAH NAMUGERWA

Born: 2004
Social media:
📷 @namugerwaleah
🐦 @leahinitiative

IRELAND

DARA McANULTY

Illustrated by
VICTORIA MADERNA
&
FEDERICO PIATTI

One of Dara's earliest memories is lying on his parents' bed...

...waiting for the golden shadow of the blackbird to appear...

...its song announcing the start of a new day.

One day the blackbird wasn't there, and Dara was devastated. The routine was gone.

It's winter! They'll be back in the spring.

Yeah?

Yes, every year.

Dara wanted to learn more about birds and nature. He began to read every fact book he could find in the library.

His family lived in the city, so nature was harder to spot, but Dara managed to find pockets of wildlife that brought him comfort in a noisy world he often found too loud. He loved examining all the details up close. When he was five, he was diagnosed as autistic.

At school, he struggled to connect with other kids and make friends, and he was constantly bullied.

HAHA!

CRUNCH

116

All of Dara's family are autistic too—his mum, Róisín; brother, Lorcan; and little sister, Bláthnaid—all except for his dad, Paul, a conservation scientist. Dara's dad knew they found the Belfast city noise unbearable, so when Dara was 9, they moved somewhere quieter.

BZZOOOO

HONK HONK

They moved to Enniskillen...

...and things changed for their family.

They let their garden grow wild to encourage wildlife.

Dara often found the world overwhelming, but in nature, his mind felt calmer.

School was still really tough for Dara, but his family's closeness and support kept him going.

Every week, their family would go for a walk in nature.

Dara would take photos and write down everything he saw.

He found writing helped him process everything, and in June 2016, when he was 12, he decided to start a nature blog. Very soon he had readers from all over the world.

Your blog is so popular, Dara! Look at all these nice comments—thousands of readers from over 30 countries!

I didn't think anyone cared about nature like I do, but WOW!

Dara wanted to do more for birds of prey, also known as raptors. He has loved them since he was 6 years old, and the persecution of these important keystone species has always angered him. He had an idea to GPS satellite tag raptors like hen harriers and buzzards. By monitoring their locations, the Northern Ireland Raptor Study Group could learn more about them and trace wildlife crime faster. Dara organized a fundraiser called Ramble for Raptors, and hiked 28 mi. across the Cuilcagh Way in January 2018 with his parents, raising over 6 thousand pounds for the Hawk Eyes Project.

Through social media, Dara was delighted to connect with so many other people who cared about the same things he did. Dara was interviewed on TV, radio, and for newspaper articles, and he was incredibly nervous! But the more he stepped out of his comfort zone, the more confident he became.

Dara appeared on the BBC, where he met naturalist and presenter Chris Packham and they became friends. In 2018, Chris organized a People's Walk for Wildlife in London, and Dara stood up on stage and spoke to over 10,000 people in Hyde Park!

In 2018, Dara began to write a book, chronicling the four seasons in a year from his fourteenth to fifteenth birthday. He also took part in the Friday School Strikes.

My name's Dara. I'm a 14-year-old naturalist and conservationist who is deeply concerned at the state of our wildlife.

We strike for people, planet, and all life on earth!

SCHOOL STRIKE 4NATURE

His family moved home again to Castlewellan, and although Dara found the change hard, he met a group of kind, nature-loving people at his new school, started an eco school club, and made a bunch of awesome friends.

When Dara's book *Diary of a Young Naturalist* was published, he became the youngest winner of the Wainwright Nature Writing Prize. He was only 16!

Still on for Xbox this weekend?

See you at Roots and Shoots!

Yeah, definitely!

It means so much to be recognized in this way, and it sends out the message that the work young people do is valuable, and that we can be part of the literature community.

When young autistic people are nurtured and accepted, miraculous things can happen, and this is certainly one of them. Thank you so much.

My message to everyone is to just *get out into nature.* It will benefit your life so, so much. Take those 5 minutes a day just to *notice* the world around you. Because by *noticing,* we build up this picture of our world that inspires *connection* and *love* and *compassion.* And from that, we build up a *determination* to want to protect [nature]. And by everyone wanting to protect that, *together* we can make real change in the world.

WHAT ARE THEY DOING NOW?

Dara has worked with the the Royal Society for the Protection of Birds (RSPB), the Wildlife Trust, and the National Trust. He has written for many publications and appeared on BBC *Springwatch* with Chris Packham and BBC *Countryfile* and presented radio for BBC Ulster Radio. He is proudly open about being autistic and describing how nature helped him and uses his platform to empower others.

Dara's blog won the youth category in Wildlife Trust's 30 Days Wild campaign, and the Best Blog of 2016 award from A Focus on Nature. In 2017, Dara was awarded the BBC *Springwatch* Unsprung Hero Award, *Birdwatch* magazine's Local Hero Award, and the Chief Scout Award for his service to environmental work. In 2018, Dara became an ambassador for the RSPCA and the iWill Campaign, and in 2019, he became a young ambassador for the Jane Goodall Institute. Dara was the youngest ever recipient of the RSPB Medal for Conservation for his raptor conservation work and raising awareness of biodiversity loss. In 2020, at age 16, Dara was the youngest author to be long-listed for the Baillie Gifford Prize for nonfiction, and to be shortlisted for the Books are My Bag Readers Award.

Dara volunteers for various causes, including recording local red squirrel sightings, monitoring hen harriers, and helping his dad care for rescue bats as a young bat worker. He also makes nature and wildlife awareness displays for schools and organizations.

Dara continues to campaign for the environment and

write books, engaging with and nurturing our connection to nature. "My passion is involving young people, showing my excitement for nature and seeing their eyes light up too—it's magical and necessary if we are going to solve the many ecological problems we now face."

In 2022, Dara began studying natural sciences at the University of Cambridge.

"Hope is what *drives* us to action
and motivates us to take action.
Because without hope,
why would we bother if we did not
believe we could succeed.
And so hope is *essential*, and going out
into nature is the bringer of that hope."
—DARA McANULTY

Born: 2004
Website: daramcanulty.com
Social media:
 @dara_mcanulty
 @NaturalistDara
Publications: *Wild Child: Nature Adventures for Young Explorers*, *Wild Child: A Journey Through Nature*, *A Wild Child's Book of Birds*, *Diary of a Young Naturalist*

WHAT CAN YOU DO?

When asking *What can I do?*, it's really important to think about this quote from writer, historian, and activist Rebecca Solnit:

"A climate story we urgently need is one that exposes who is actually responsible for climate chaos . . . Oxfam reports that over the past twenty-five years, the carbon impact of the top 1 percent of the wealthiest human beings was twice that of the bottom 50 percent . . . By saying 'we are all responsible,' we avoid the fact that the global majority of us don't need to change much, but a minority needs to change a lot."

It's also important to remember how effective the propaganda of fossil fuel giant BP was in coining the phrase "carbon footprint," which shifted the responsibility to the individual, and away from the fossil fuel companies responsible for the crisis in the first place.

So, bearing this in mind, there absolutely *are* things you can do as an individual, working in communities and raising your voice, that can make a huge difference, just like the activists in this book. And this doesn't mean that making individual lifestyle changes is pointless—it can have a domino effect on others changing too. When facing this crisis, we all need to hold our world leaders to account in protecting and restoring nature and moving away from fossil fuels, and at the same time we absolutely need individual change that inspires shifts in culture and society.

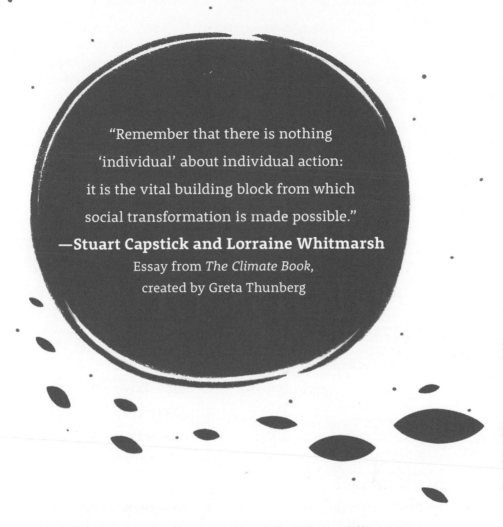

"Remember that there is nothing 'individual' about individual action: it is the vital building block from which social transformation is made possible."

—Stuart Capstick and Lorraine Whitmarsh

Essay from *The Climate Book*,
created by Greta Thunberg

The best way to start is with one achievable goal (for example, signing up to a community action group, cutting out beef, or committing to only buying sustainable or thrifted clothes you'll wear for years) and go from there. It's not about being a "perfect" person or holding others to that standard. Be kind to others, whatever stage they're at, and remember, everyone has a different level of privilege and can't always make the same changes you can.

Here are some things you can do as an individual:

Diet

Shifting to a plant-based diet is one of the most impactful changes you can make as an individual, with cutting out beef being number one. Shop seasonally and locally where possible and avoid plastic packaging as much as you can. Choose organic foods if your budget allows, as they avoid chemical pesticides, which benefits the soil and the wider animal food chain.

Things we own

Think about what you're buying and if you really need it. For example, think about if you need a new phone every eighteen months, or if clever advertising and capitalism are just telling you that. Reuse, repair, and recycle technology and things you own wherever possible. Beware of greenwashing, where brands make misleading claims to consumers about being eco-friendly

Clothes

Fast fashion is one of the most polluting industries, with ten thousand items ending up in landfills every five minutes. The most important thing you can do is buy fewer clothes in general. Wherever you can, try to buy things you will wear for years, not days. Try thrifting and shopping secondhand, clothes swaps with friends, and repairing clothes. Avoid clothes that are made of plastics (like polyester and nylon), which shed microplastics when washed. Instead, opt for materials like 100 percent cotton (certified organic if possible) and other natural biodegradable fabrics.

Litter and plastic

Removing plastic and litter where you live helps rivers, oceans, communities, and animals all over the world. There is no "away." Your litter will just end up somewhere else, so always recycle and dispose responsibly. Refuse plastic wherever you can. There is a limited amount of times plastic can be recycled, and most can't be recycled at all. Use a reusable drinking bottle, but if you have to go single-use, choose aluminum/tin cans or glass—they have a cyclical recycling loop, meaning no new virgin materials are needed to make more, and they can be recycled forever!

Divest your money

Check if your bank invests in fossil fuel companies and move to a greener bank if they do. Check with the bill payer which energy company your household uses, and switch to a green energy supplier that uses clean renewable energy to power your home rather than fossil fuels.

Transportation

Take public transport, walk, or cycle instead of driving where possible. Fly less or wait for electric planes to be commonplace.

Water

Flush the toilet less (pee in the shower!) and try to conserve water wherever possible.

Nature and wildlife

If you have a garden, allow it to grow wild. Avoid pesticides and give insects and the wider food chain a chance. Encourage and support community projects for rewilding. Beware of mass tree-planting schemes that have a monoculture (one type of tree). Make sure they say "diverse and native" and are a genuine charity.

Use your skills!

Share your knowledge and educate others! Maybe you're an artist? A musician? Passionate about wildlife? Use your talents, your platform, and contact your network of people you know (however small it may seem) to spread the word! There are many wonderful existing organizations that need your help, like the ones in this book. Sign up and get involved!

"We keep fighting
because that is our only option,
and we have to hold on to hope.
A hope rooted in action."

—Jamie Margolin

DEFEND THE DEFENDERS
BY JAMIE MARGOLIN

I began my work in the climate movement in 2016, when I was fourteen, and I'm twenty now as I'm writing this. It's weird to feel so cynical at my age, but when you spend your adolescence experiencing in painful firsthand how badly governments are failing to tackle the biggest challenge humans have faced, it's hard not to be.

How do we just go about our regular lives like normal under the weight of knowing what is going on? And yet we do, I do, because we just have to keep going. Giving up is accepting defeat, handing our whole earth up to climate chaos on a silver platter. We keep fighting because that is our only option, and we have to hold on to hope. A hope rooted in action. After years of going to event after event, conference after conference, protest after protest, meeting after meeting, I've learned we have to see through what is fake and focus on the actual tangible solutions.

There is so much corporate greenwashing now that the climate movement has become considered mainstream. Even fossil fuel corporations have environmental-type messaging in their ads, despite being a main cause of climate disaster. When a movement becomes popular enough, corporations and governments sweep in to look like they're doing the right thing, but it doesn't take much digging to see it's an advertising facade.

Globally we need to learn from and protect those who have not lost that connection to the earth, even after centuries of colonization. When it comes to protecting life on earth, our success will depend on how much attention, energy, resources, and support we give to those on the front lines.

Eighty percent of the world's biodiversity is protected by Indigenous peoples. Between 2012 and 2022, 1,733 defenders have been killed trying to protect their land. The people who are facing the worst consequences of the global capitalist extraction at the root of the climate crisis are the least responsible for the climate crisis, and yet the most harmed. Those who do everything they can to defend their homelands from destruction are often persecuted by their own governments and those who protect corporate interests.

Not nearly enough attention and resources from those around the world who care about the climate crisis are going to the people who do the most to defend our planet. Most global climate funding goes to large nonprofits with already formidable budgets, and most mainstream news outlets do not sufficiently (if at all) cover what is happening on the last lines of defense of our planet.

I imagine the fight we are in right now as a battle between two ultimate overarching forces—those who are fighting for the interests of those destroying life on earth, and those of us who fight to protect life on earth. If we're thinking of this fight like a battleground, then the land and water defenders are the people on the very front lines of it. The lack of resources, support, media attention, and overall global mobilization to do everything we can to support people involved in the climate fight is akin to dedicating most of your war resources to the people working behind a desk who never see a day of combat and leaving your front-line troops with a measly fraction.

Let's unite to support the front lines—from the land defenders in the Amazon rain forest protecting their territories from extraction to organizers facing environmental racism.

No matter where you are in the world, there are communities being impacted by extraction, mining, and the effects of the climate crisis. Do what you can locally and beyond, join communities and coalitions fighting to stop fossil fuels, learn from and support environmental defenders. Now is the time to fight strategically and ferociously, like we're fighting for our lives—because we are.

INTERVIEW WITH MELATI WIJSEN AND JAMIE MARGOLIN

Emma: I'm honored to speak with two climate activists who are featured in this book: Melati Wijsen, activist, changemaker, and cofounder of Bye Bye Plastic Bags and YOUTHTOPIA, and Jamie Margolin, Colombian/Jewish (Ashkenazi) lesbian activist, cofounder of Zero Hour, and author of *Youth to Power*.

You've both been activists for a long time. Like many of the activists in this book, you started in your youth and are now an adult. How has your view of activism shifted over time, and is there any advice you'd give to your younger self?

Melati: I have learned so much since starting at age twelve! My best advice would be a few things! It's important to keep your narrative as clear and short as possible, have a timeline with end goals, and surround yourself with a good team and support system, because it won't always be easy!

Emma: What is your most important goal for the climate justice movement?

Jamie: Stopping fascism, protecting democracy and freedom, protecting land rights and sovereignty for Indigenous peoples, halting all fossil fuel infrastructure, a just transition . . . there's no one goal that's more important, all these things must be accomplished alongside each other. We are in a race against time; it's all hands on deck.

Melati: EDUCATION! I believe that change can start in the classroom. Once we know the problem, we can create solutions and prepare how to adapt and become resilient to the changes that are coming. I strongly believe that we need to start preparing young people, and the education system needs to join the climate justice movement more boldly!

Emma: Do you have a message for global leaders?

Jamie: Despite having all the resources in the world to know better, you're selling out the world to the fossil fuel industry. You are actively destroying all life on earth and perpetuating the sixth mass extinction.

In order to prevent the world from becoming the worst-case scenario of what it can be, you need to immediately halt all fossil fuel extraction, all new fossil fuel infrastructure, and fund a just transition both locally and globally so that those worst impacted by the climate crisis in the Global South and in specific climate-impacted communities have resources they need. Land rights and sovereignty and respect for their territories must be given to all Indigenous peoples around the world—justice for Indigenous people is climate justice.

So many lives have already been ended and uprooted

because of the climate crisis, and the climate crisis is a problem created by corporations and governments. Corporations and governments are run by human beings. It's a handful of humans at the top consistently making the choice to burn the planet and destroy life as we know it.

If you have any humanity in you at all, any soul, any sense of right or wrong, any love for this world or your children—you will do everything necessary to combat the climate crisis.

Melati: Young people are more than an inspiration only! Our generation is one of the biggest untapped sources for solutions! Invite us into the decision-making rooms and allow us to help implement the new systemic changes we need to see.

Emma: The climate and nature crisis can be overwhelming and scary—how do you stay calm and manage your climate anxiety?

Jamie: Live in the present. Honestly, sometimes you just have to turn off your phone, turn off the news, spend time with people you care about or do something you love or just sit in the current moment you're in, whatever it is, and unplug from thinking about massive issues beyond any of our individual control. This doesn't mean permanently hide from the world and throw your hands up and never try to change anything, but balance and time away from thinking about all this stuff (if that is a privilege you have; I'm aware for those in the midst of experiencing climate-related life complications, you can't really not think about it).

For me personally, fiction is how I manage my anxiety and escape. Specifically, animated fictional shows and movies, as well as comics and novels. I disappear into the worlds of *Arcane, Avatar: The Last Airbender, The Legend of Korra, She-Ra and the Princesses of Power*, comforting animated Disney movies like *Frozen I* and *II, Encanto*, and the worlds of my favorite Studio Ghibli movies, like *Spirited Away* and *Kiki's Delivery Service*. Well-crafted animated stories transport me to another world and are the part of me that remains uncynical, that has joy and wonder that I won't let go of. Everyone has hobbies and things they like to do, stories they like to disappear into, people they like to spend time with, and for as long as we have whatever it is we have that brings us joy, we need to take time to enjoy it with those we love.

Melati: Yes, it does get quite overwhelming! I think the way I stay grounded is by remembering that I am not alone. There are so many of us doing such incredible work. So when it feels overwhelming and when your immediate surroundings are slow to change, sometimes it helps to celebrate the accomplishments of others who were able to achieve tangible change! We can do this!

And of course, living on the island of Bali also means I get to go on frequent walks in nature—this really calms my anxiety and helps manage my mood!

Emma: My hope comes from knowing activism has worked throughout history in changing the world for the better, and imagining a rewilded and equitable future for nature and humans. What does a hopeful future world look like for you?

Jamie: We can't control the disastrous global warming already locked into our planet's atmosphere and the unravelling of ecosystems that are already coming undone, but we can stop making the problem worse by ending all fossil fuel extraction and use, switching completely to renewable energy, stopping all deforestation, and making sure we maintain free democracies and prevent wars and fascism.

As planetary systems continue to unravel, we must be vigilant in participating in democracies, protecting democracies, protecting free and fair elections, and stopping fascists or any pro-war, anti-climate politician. Climate scientist Katharine Hayhoe has said what is needed is realism, action, and hope. "It's really bad and there's a good chance that it will get worse," Hayhoe has said for a report for AP. "But if we do everything we can, that will make a difference. Our actions will make the difference . . . That's what hope is."

Melati: A hopeful future world to me is powered by the sun, has clean rivers and lakes that become the source for our plastic-free water, has inclusive and diverse leadership, and has classrooms that empower and prepare youth to deal with the upcoming challenges and opportunities! For me a hopeful future is one where everyone feels content, not left behind, and believes that they have the ability to create positive change!

Melati: We LOVE using art as a medium for change because art has no barriers! Much like activism, art can make people feel moved. And it's a beautiful way to share a message that sometimes words cannot translate properly!

Jamie: Art has an ability to rapidly and universally communicate messages. Art is everywhere—from the protest signs and banners that were designed and created with much thought and intention for every action you see, to the films big and small that highlight important issues, to the art of music, performance, murals, paintings—the list goes on. Art gives us joy, it gives us entertainment, it helps us relate to, understand, and empathize with information, people, and experiences we wouldn't have otherwise had a connection to.

Art in the movement is a vessel for communicating information, for helping people understand concepts in a more universal way, to share emotions, and to cope and express the pain and anxiety that comes with living during the sixth mass extinction.

Art is what gives me joy, hope, and purpose in moments where everything feels dark. I am in the process of creating an animated film, *Pelea*, that is a fictionalized version of fighting against fossil fuel extraction. It is a long way away from completion, as animation is time-consuming and my team and I at Pelea Animation are making sure we get this film right. Right now, that is how I am combining my determination to fight for climate justice and my love for writing, directing, and animation. Storytelling is an important art form, and I am happy to devote my life to being a storyteller.

Emma: What advice would you give to people who are now starting their activism journey?

Melati: Find your focus! Changemaking can feel overwhelming, but if you know your vision clearly, it's easier to keep on going! Aside from this, if your vision of change is clear, it will also be easier to mobilize people and achieve your goals! And of course, remember that you cannot do it on your own! Surround yourself with a team who can help take your ideas, your vision, and turn it into reality!

Jamie: Work in community, work with others who also understand the severity of the climate crisis and have common goals as you. If you go on this journey alone, it can quickly get incredibly isolating, taxing, and you can burn out or fall into despair shouldering the burden of fighting for something so intense alone. The climate crisis is a systemic issue caused by governments and corporations working together to profit at humanity's expense, so we need to organize in mass collectives to be able to oppose them and switch the world to renewable energy and a just transition. Work in community, whether that be with an organization, a community group or coalition, or even just a group of people in your circles who want to take action, and come together to do it. It can be overwhelming starting your activism journey, but it's important work, and there's no better way to learn how to take action than to dive in and start working with other people taking climate action. Learn as you go, learn from those around you with more experience, and make sure to keep your eyes on what you're fighting for.

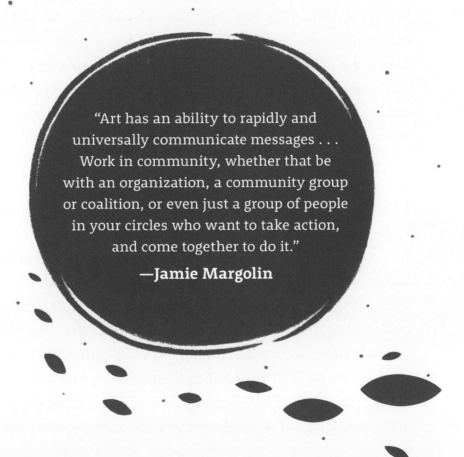

"Art has an ability to rapidly and universally communicate messages . . . Work in community, whether that be with an organization, a community group or coalition, or even just a group of people in your circles who want to take action, and come together to do it."

—Jamie Margolin

WHAT IS THE IPCC REPORT?

The IPCC (Intergovernmental Panel on Climate Change) is the United Nations body responsible for assessing the science related to climate change.

The IPCC are climate experts who read through thousands of research papers by climate scientists from around the world. These are thoroughly fact-checked, and then the key findings are used to make the IPCC report. The reports are independent, impartial, and the most reliable source of information available in the world, so the information in the reports can be used by governments to develop climate policies.

Each report has three sections. Working Group I: The Physical Science Basis of Climate Change; Working Group II: Climate Change Impacts, Adaptation, and Vulnerability; and Working Group III: Mitigation of Climate Change.

It's important to know the difference between the full report, which is thousands of pages written by expert climate scientists, and the "Report Summary," which has to be approved by politicians. We can trust the IPCC scientists and the full report, but just be wary of the "summary."

Founded in 1988, the IPCC releases reports every six or seven years, and sometimes do special reports in between, such as the "Global Warming of 1.5°C" impact report in October 2018. This report showed the world that we need to take drastic action to reduce global heating and limit the temperature rise to 1.5 degrees Celsius (rather than a devastating

2 degrees) by reaching net zero on CO_2 by 2050.

It also said that we have just over ten years to limit the most devastating effects of climate change. This 2018 report and urgent timeline was a pivotal moment in public awareness of the climate crisis, and made headlines worldwide. The youth climate strikes accelerated this movement, until soon the climate crisis and calls on leaders to take action was a household conversation that could no longer be ignored.

The sixth IPCC report was published in 2022, and gives an eight-to-nine-year deadline for taking urgent action to ensure a livable future, recognizing that marginalized communities are the most affected. The April 2022 IPCC mitigation report said that if global carbon emissions are halved by 2030, there is still a chance of staying within the crucial 1.5 degrees Celsius of global warming. The key ways to do this are to rapidly phase out fossil fuels and scale up renewable energy capacity, and to transform how we manage land. For the first time, the IPCC acknowledged that colonialism is a historical and ongoing driver of climate change, and that individual behavior is important but that systemic changes are needed to encourage and support this behavior.

The Paris Agreement

The fifth IPCC report in 2014 led to all 196 countries in the world meeting to discuss the scientific findings at the Paris Conference in 2015. An agreement was finally reached, called "The Paris Agreement," which was signed on Earth Day, April 22, 2016.

This historic agreement was a promise to reduce carbon

emissions as soon as possible, with a goal to limit global warming to 2 degrees Celsius (preferably 1.5 degrees Celsius) above preindustrial* levels.

By January 2021, 195 countries had signed and 190 countries had ratified the agreement (made it official).

What is the COP?

The COP (Conference of the Parties) is a yearly United Nations climate change conference that began in 1995. The aim of the COP is to review the progress toward the UNFCCC (United Nations Framework Convention on Climate Change)—a voluntary agreement between the countries of the United Nations with a goal to limit climate change.

In 1972, the United Nations Conference on the Human Environment (UNCHE) produced the Stockholm Declaration, a revolutionary document on important global environmental issues that didn't put business interests first.

> "In the 20 years between the UNCHE and the 1992 Rio Earth summit, which was the precursor to what we now call [COP,] the business community fully infiltrated international discussions on environmental issues and successfully moved the goalposts. Gone was the emphasis on government regulation, replaced by [an] . . . approach that included business interests and prioritized compromise . . . "
> **—Amy Westervelt**
> Print and environmental journalist, runs *Critical Frequency* and *Drilled* podcasts and cohosts *Hot Take* podcast and newsletter

The positives of COP are that it exists at all, and that climate change is being discussed on a global scale, and previous COPs have been the biggest gathering of world leaders. However, there has not been enough urgent progress made since it began over twenty-five years ago, namely because of the huge attendance of people in the fossil fuel industry.

> "You can't negotiate an effective climate solution when your conference is full of fossil fuel lobbyists. If the fossil fuel industry were a country, it would have had more reps at COP than any other country in the world."
>
> **—Amy Westervelt**

Youth activists also describe a great deal of "youth-washing"—where they are invited to COP "for show," but not given a seat at the decision-making table. Activists also face racism and a lack of proper representation for marginalized groups, and this needs to change.

---

*preindustrial: Referring to a period of time before the start of the Industrial Revolution. The Industrial Revolution was between 1760–1840 and is when humans began to burn vast amounts of fossil fuels, causing carbon emissions to rise dramatically.

TIMELINE OF SIGNIFICANT CLIMATE EVENTS 1760–2007

1760–1840 – A boom in invention of machinery called the Industrial Revolution occurs. Humans begin to burn vast amounts of fossil fuels to run industrial machines in factories and steamships and trains powered by coal.

1879 – Thomas Edison invents the electric light bulb, but many people continue to use gas lamps and candles for another fifty years.

1890s – Early observations of the greenhouse effect.

1903 – First airplane invented by the Wright Brothers.

1907 – First synthetic plastic invented.

1914–1918 – World War I.

1928–1933 – The Great Depression.

1930s – Wind generators for electricity common on farms, mostly in the US.

1933 – Polyethylene, a now common type of plastic, is accidentally developed.

1939–1945 – World War II.

1950s – Plastic use increases, including popularity of single-use eating utensils, microwave meals, and the fast food industry in the US, spreading worldwide by the '70s.

1954–1968 – The American Civil Rights movement.

1958 – US starts using nuclear power. NASA founded.

1960s – Peak of world oil field discoveries, totaling around 55 billion barrels' worth in volume.

1961 – World Wildlife Foundation (WWF) is founded.

1962 – Rachel Carson's groundbreaking book *Silent Spring* is released, warning of the effects of then commonly used DDT, an incredibly dangerous man-made pesticide.

1965 – Scientists first voice concerns about the greenhouse effect causing the earth to heat because of increasing carbon dioxide.

1966 – US and Western Europe begin intensive animal factory farming, with other nations joining over the next twenty years.

1969 – Moon landing: first man lands on the moon.

1970s – Fossil fuel companies begin their propaganda to deny climate change and confuse the public and government policy.

1970 – First Earth Day, inspired by student-led antiwar protests.

1971 – Greenpeace is founded.

1972 – United Nations Conference on the Human Environment (UNCHE) in Stockholm, Europe—first world conference to make the environment a major issue.

1975 – The term *global warming* is coined and popularized by geochemist Wallace Broecker.

1984 – Wallace Broecker calls for urgent political action to stop greenhouse gases building up.

1988 – The Intergovernmental Panel on Climate Change (IPCC) is formed.

1989 – Record-breaking heat waves make headlines worldwide and are linked to global warming.

1990s – Scientific community overwhelmingly agrees that human-caused greenhouse emissions are responsible for climate changes and global warming.

1992 – The Rio Earth Summit.

1994 – The internet becomes popular. Cell phones, home computers, and video game consoles also boom.

1995 – First COP (Conference of the Parties), yearly United Nations climate change conferences.

1997 – The Kyoto Protocol is signed.

2000s – Fossil fuel companies continue their propaganda. BP invests huge sums in public relations advertising to coin the term *carbon footprint* to place the blame on individual responsibility rather than huge companies doing damage and producing millions of barrels of fossil fuels every day.

2000 – World's first commercial wave power device is installed on the Scottish coast.

2005 – First Global Day of Action takes place during the Montreal Climate Change Conference in December. Thousands of international events take place in over twenty countries, and they continue to take place every year around COP.

2005 – Installing solar panels on houses becomes popular.

2006 – Al Gore's environmental documentary *An Inconvenient Truth* is released, raising international public awareness of climate change.

2007 – 350.org international environmental organization founded.

TIMELINE OF SIGNIFICANT CLIMATE EVENTS 2010-2023, INCLUDING THE ACTIVISTS IN THIS BOOK

2010

Floods in Pakistan; Iqbal Badruddin Jamal begins his activism.

2011

International student groups campaign for their universities to divest from (stop investing in) fossil fuels, with great success over the next decade.

2012

Autumn Peltier begins her activism after seeing the boil water advisories in Serpent River.

2013

Bye Bye Plastic Bags is founded by Melati and Isabel Wijsen.

Black Lives Matter founded.

Tokata begins activism—testifies against a uranium mine in the sacred Black Hills.

2014

Pacific Climate Warriors, a Pacific Island state grassroots movement for climate justice, peacefully blocks the world's largest coal port in Newcastle, Australia.

2015

Edgar Edmund Tarimo begins inventing.

The Paris Agreement is agreed (comes into force November 4, 2016).

2016

In early 2016, the #NoDAPL movement begins. In June, Tokata and Indigenous youth form ReZpect Our Water.

Zero Hour is founded by Jamie Margolin, Nadia Nazar, Madelaine Tew, and Zanagee Artis. Jerome Foster II joins Zero Hour.

Dara McAnulty starts his nature blog.

Assembly of First Nations annual winter meeting—Autumn Peltier confronts President Trudeau.

2017

The Sunrise Movement is founded.

Blue Planet II documentary airs on the BBC. The "Attenborough effect" encourages a huge number of people to change their behavior and reduce plastic pollution.

Ridhima Pandey begins activism by filing petition against government in India.

Jean Hinchliffe begins volunteering for the "Vote Yes" marriage equality campaign.

2018

February – Parkland school shooting in the US. Daphne Frias begins her gun violence activism.

March – March for Our Lives (MFOL), US student-led march in support of gun control legislation.

May – Extinction Rebellion founded.

July 21 – Youth Climate March. Zero Hour and their ally groups march in Washington, DC, US.

August – School Strike for Climate: Fridays for Future is founded by Greta Thunberg in Sweden.

October – IPCC report gives a twelve-year deadline to avoid the worst impacts of climate change, making headlines around the world.

November – Jean Hinchliffe helps organize School Strike 4 Climate with 15,000 protestors in Australia.

December – Fridays for Future Pakistan founded by Iqbal Badruddin Jamal.

2019

February 8 – Leah Namugerwa begins her Friday school strikes in Uganda. Leah and fellow activists form Fridays for Future Uganda.

February 28 – #KidLit4Climate is founded by Emma Reynolds in Manchester, UK. Children's illustrators and authors from around the world create a viral online art campaign in solidarity with youth climate strikers—the first global art campaign for the climate crisis.

March 15 – First Global Climate Strike!

May 16 – Ōu Hóngyì becomes first youth climate protestor in Mainland China.

May 24 – Second Global Climate Strike!

Summer – Arshak Makichyan and fellow activists form Fridays for Future Russia.

September 20–27 – Global Week for Future.

September 20 – All-ages Global Climate Strike—a historic day, the biggest day of global climate action to date.

November 29 – Strike before COP25—two million people across 157 countries.

2020

January 30 – Novel coronavirus declared Global Health Emergency by WHO. Named COVID-19 on February 11, 2020.

March 11 – Greta Thunberg urges strikers to strike online using #ClimateStrikeOnline to stay safe as COVID-19 spreads.

June – Black Lives Matter civil rights protests sparked by the murders of George Floyd, Breonna Taylor, and Ahmaud Arbery.

September 25 – Global Climate Strike.

2021

March 19 – Global Climate Strike: #NoMoreEmptyPromises.

April – CarbonTracker.org report states that solar and wind energy potential is over one hundred times more than global energy demand—and cheaper too, far outweighing fossil fuel efficiency.

September 24 – Global Climate Strike.

2022

Record hot temperatures across the world during 2022, including the tropics and polar regions.

January – In California, Save the Redwoods League hands back a 532-acre redwood forest to Native American tribe descendants to conserve.

February 24 – Russia invades Ukraine.

Due to the conflict in Ukraine, the International Energy Agency predicts for the first time that global demand for fossil fuels will peak in the mid-2030s.

March – Joining New Zealand, Ecuador, and Mexico, Panama introduces a rights of nature law.

March 3 – At UN Environment Assembly, 175 nations agree to end plastic waste in a landmark deal.

April – In response to the latest IPCC report, over 1,000 scientists from 25 countries take part in the Scientist Rebellion's protests and demonstrations.

September 15 – In a historic move, billionaire Yvon Chouinard, founder of outdoor clothing brand Patagonia, announces he will be giving away all the company's profits in order to invest in fighting the climate crisis.

September 23 – Global Climate Strike.

November – COP27 delegates pledge to set up a "loss and damage" fund to pay reparations to poorer countries that are bearing the brunt of the climate crisis but have historically contributed the least emissions and damage.

December – Scientists at California's Lawrence Livermore National Laboratory make a major breakthrough in clean nuclear fusion energy, which doesn't produce damaging radioactive waste like current nuclear power plants.

December 20 – At the UN Biodiversity Conference (COP15), almost two hundred nations agree to a landmark milestone deal to preserve 30 percent of Earth for nature.

2023

United Nations report finds that the hole in Earth's ozone layer should be fully healed over most of the world by 2040.

January 1 – The president of Brazil, Jair Bolsonaro, is voted out, and Lula da Silva is inaugurated, vowing to protect the Amazon rain forest from deforestation, which was accelerated under Bolsonaro.

February 7 – A report by Climate Power finds that the Inflation Reduction Act in the US successfully created over 100,000 clean energy jobs in less than six months.

February 8 – Historic first—Australia's environment minister, Tanya Plibersek, blocks a new coal mine near the Great Barrier Reef.

February 9 – ClientEarth sues individual members of fossil fuel giant Shell's board of directors for "failing to adopt and implement an energy transition strategy that aligns with the Paris Agreement."

March 3 – Global Climate Strike: End Fossil Finance.

March 4 – Nations reach a historic agreement to protect the world's oceans. The High Seas Treaty will place 30 percent of the seas in protected areas by 2030, so nature can recover.

March 13 – US president Biden approves Willow, the colossal, controversial oil drilling project in Alaska, betraying his climate promise to move away from fossil fuels.

In early 2023, fossil fuel giants including BP and Shell reported that 2022 was their highest earning year ever, raking in billions in profit.

"We must change course.
The only credible direction to take is away from fossil fuels and toward renewable energy."

—António Guterres,
Secretary-General of the United Nations

FURTHER READING, WATCHING, AND LISTENING

There are tons of resources and organizations out there where you can learn more about the climate and nature crisis and how to be an activist. Here are just some of them that I recommend:

FOR AN EMPOWERING INTRODUCTION TO THE CLIMATE AND NATURE CRISIS:

Climate Crisis for Beginners by Andy Prentice and Eddie Reynolds, illustrated by El Primo Ramon
A brilliant introduction to the science and what we can do about the climate crisis, with engaging illustrations.

The Climate Book by Greta Thunberg
Essays written by Greta and over one hundred experts from all around the world on everything we need to know—including the science, intersectional solutions, and the changes in systems and society that need to happen.

aimhi.earth
Accessible climate education courses equipping people and organizations with the essential understanding, skills, and ideas to overcome the climate and nature crisis and ensure a healthier, fairer future. Cofounded by environmentalist and scientist Matthew Shribman, the team are nature-first thinkers, at the forefront of accelerating the learning process

by blending science, psychology, storytelling, and design—leading to rapid understanding and motivation to take action.

FOR VITAL INTERSECTIONAL SOLUTIONS:

indigenousclimateaction.com

Indigenous-led organization working to inspire and support Indigenous climate action.

intersectionalenvironmentalist.com

A climate justice collective radically imagining a more equitable and diverse future of environmentalism, founded by Leah Thomas, aka GreenGirlLeah. Check out her excellent book: *The Intersectional Environmentalist: How to Dismantle Systems of Oppression to Protect People + Planet.*

All We Can Save: Truth, Courage, and Solutions for the Climate Crisis edited by Dr. Ayana Elizabeth Johnson and Dr. Katharine Wilkinson

A bestselling anthology of writing by sixty women at the forefront of the climate movement who are harnessing truth, courage, and solutions to lead humanity forward. Check out Dr. Ayana Elizabeth Johnson's ClimateVenn.info too.

earthrise.studio

Earthrise is a collective of designers, filmmakers, and writers dedicated to communicating how we navigate the climate crisis by sharing radical stories of hope and new possibility. Check out their website articles and Instagram posts for a series of great intersectional climate justice resources.

It's Not That Radical: Climate Action to
Transform Our World **by Mikaela Loach**

In her book, Michaela Loach highlights harmful systems of oppression, exposing the root causes of the climate crisis. A radical, hopeful, and accessible approach to taking action for intersectional climate justice.

INITIATIVES FOR EMPOWERING DIVERSITY IN ENJOYING NATURE AND THE OUTDOORS:

Protecting and restoring nature for all is vital to combat the climate crisis, but outdoor pursuits in nature as well as working in sciences are very white spaces, and this needs to change.

brownpeoplecamping.com

A social media initiative that advocates for greater diversity, equity, access, and social justice in the outdoors. Check out the hashtag #BrownPeopleCamping and also #OutdoorsForAll.

disabledhikers.com

Building disability community and justice in the outdoors, with a vision to transform outdoor culture through representation, access, and justice for disabled and all other marginalized people.

unlikelyhikers.org

A diverse, antiracist, body-liberating outdoor community featuring the underrepresented outdoorsperson. They have an Instagram community, a nationwide hiking group, and a podcast.

blackafinstem.com

Supporting, uplifting, and amplifying Black STEM (science, technology, engineering, mathematics) professionals in natural resources and the environment through professional development, career connection, and community engagement. They run #BlackBirdersWeek.

HOW YOU CAN ALSO BE A
YOUNG CHANGEMAKER:

youthtopia.world

A global project to empower youth through engaging peer-to-peer education, founded by Melati and Isabel Wijsen.

Youth to Power: Your Voice and How to Use It
by Jamie Margolin

A guide to being an activist and maintaining a healthy activist-life balance.

PODCASTS:

The Joy Report

Sharing stories about climate solutions and environmental justice grounded in intersectionality, optimism, and joy: intersectionalenvironmentalist.com/the-joy-report

The Happy Broadcast Podcast

Listen to positive news collected from around the world, along with mental health tips and listener community voices: thehappybroadcast.com/podcast

AND FINALLY:

Despite what the mainstream news may lead you to believe, good things are happening too. Did you know that bad news gets more clicks and attention, and therefore makes more money for news media through advertising revenue? So it's vital that, alongside acknowledging the climate crisis unfolding, we are aware of the amazing progress being made too.

positive.news

Print magazine and website with articles by independent journalists, focusing on solutions and highlighting social and environmental progress and positive news.

Good News: Why the World Is Not as Bad as You Think by Rashmi Sirdeshpande, illustrated by Adam Hayes

This inspiring book highlights that there are good things happening in the world, even if we don't hear about them as much. It also equips you with the tools to suss out what is fake news and what isn't.

thehappybroadcast.com

The Happy Broadcast celebrates and illustrates positive climate and other news from all around the world. Hope and optimism are vital in this fight!

GLOSSARY

Ableism – Discrimination against people with disabilities and favoring of nondisabled people.

Ambulatory – Able to walk.

Autism – Being born autistic isn't an illness or disease that needs a cure—it is a lifelong disability affecting how autistic people communicate and interact with the world. It is a spectrum—and different autistic people have different strengths and need different levels of support.

Biodegradable – Something that can be decomposed (broken down) naturally by bacteria, fungi, or other living organisms, making it ecologically harmless.

Biodiversity – The variety of life on earth, made up of a variation and balanced ecosystem of plants, animals, fungi, and microorganisms working together.

Capitalism – A system where trade and industry are owned by private companies, focused on making a profit above all else.

Carbon budget – A limit on how much carbon dioxide (CO_2) can be emitted over a certain time period.

Carbon footprint – The greenhouse gas emissions caused by an individual person, group of people, product, or company. The term *carbon footprint* was coined by oil and gas company BP, who invested huge sums in public relations advertising in the 2000s to place the blame on individual responsibility rather than huge companies doing the damage and producing millions of barrels of fossil fuels every day.

Carbon sink – Something that absorbs and stores carbon from the atmosphere. Our biggest natural carbon sinks are plants, soil, and the ocean.

Carbon source – Something that releases carbon into the atmosphere, like burning fossil fuels or a forest fire. The opposite of a carbon sink.

Climate (and climate change) – Climate is the long-term average weather and temperature of a place, whereas weather is more day-to-day changes. Climate change is these long-term averages changing dramatically, e.g., shorter, warmer winters and record-breaking temperatures in summer causing drought.

Climate anxiety (also called eco-anxiety) – Anxiety related to the climate and nature crisis.

Climate change denial – The denial of the scientific community's consensus that climate change and global warming exist and are being caused by humans burning too many fossil fuels and destroying nature.

Climate literacy – An educational understanding of the climate—being "climate literate."

CO_2 – Carbon dioxide, a greenhouse gas that is released into the atmosphere when burning fossil fuels, causing global heating at an extremely fast rate.

Colonization – Violently seizing control of Indigenous, First Nations, and Aboriginal peoples, their land, and their resources, usually resulting in their exploitation and genocide.

COP (Conference of the Parties) – Yearly United Nations climate change conferences, which began in 1995.

Decarbonization – Reducing the amount of CO_2 being released into the atmosphere.

Divest – To stop investing in something—the opposite of investing.

Ecocide – "Killing one's home." *Ecocide* means unlawful or wanton acts committed with knowledge that there is a substantial likelihood of severe and either widespread or long-term damage to the environment being caused by those acts. Stopecocide.earth are working hard to make ecocide an international crime.

Environmentalism – An ideology focused on protecting the environment.

Environmental racism – Where through deliberate design rooted in systemic racism, environmental hazards disproportionately affect people of color. (Examples: building polluting factories in areas where communities of color live, building pipelines through Indigenous lands and water instead of through a white community.)

Equity – Equity is when people are treated fairly and given the resources they need to thrive based on their unique circumstances. "Equality is giving everyone the same pair of shoes. Equity is giving everyone a pair of shoes that fits."—Vernon Wall.

Fascism – A society that has a controlling government that is ruled by a dictator, where disagreeing with the government is not allowed.

Fossil fuels – Fossil fuels (such as coal) are found in Earth's crust and form naturally from decomposed animals and plants. The carbon cycle is a natural process, but humans are disrupting this cycle by unearthing and then burning vast amounts of fossil fuels.

Global North – A term to describe a group of countries broadly characterized as wealthy and powerful. It does not refer to the whole northern hemisphere geographically.

Global South – A term to describe a group of lower-income countries, many of which are or were colonized. It does not refer to the whole southern hemisphere geographically.

Global warming/heating – The process of the global temperature increasing because of humans burning vast amounts of fossil fuels and destroying nature, releasing too much CO_2 and other greenhouse gases, causing the earth to heat too quickly.

Grassroots – A grassroots organization or society is run by ordinary people, not leaders.

Greenwashing – Where companies and brands make misleading claims to consumers about being eco-friendly in order to appear "green" and make money.

Indigenous peoples, First Nations, Aboriginal peoples – People descended directly from the earliest people who originally lived in a place and maintain their culture.

Industrial Revolution – Between 1760–1840, there was a boom in invention of machinery. As a result, humans began to burn vast amounts of fossil fuels to run industrial machines in factories and steamships and trains powered by coal.

Intersectionality – Intersectional theory is the interconnected overlap of someone's social categories such as race, gender, and class that result in their discrimination and oppression. Coined by Kimberlé Williams Crenshaw in 1989, through her lived experience as being Black and a woman.

Intersectional environmentalism – Combining equity in social justice and environmentalism, coined by Leah Thomas in 2020. Her intersectional environmentalist pledge, which detailed how to dismantle systems of oppression in the environmental movement and how to be an ally, reached over one million people and led to forming the organization of the same name: intersectionalenvironmentalist.com.

IPCC (Intergovernmental Panel on Climate Change) – The IPCC is the United Nations body responsible for assessing the science related to climate change.

IPCC report – The IPCC are climate experts who read through thousands of research papers by climate scientists from around the world. These are thoroughly fact-checked, and then the key findings are used to make the IPCC report. The reports are independent, impartial, and the most reliable source of information available in the world, so the information in the reports can be used by governments to develop climate policies.

LGBTQIA+ – Stands for Lesbian, Gay, Bisexual, Transgender, Queer, Intersex, Asexual, and Others.

Monoculture – One type of the same crop, plant, or tree.

Native (plants) – A plant that naturally exists in a place, rather than one imported from elsewhere and grown by humans.

Net zero – Reducing greenhouse gas emissions to zero, or as close as possible.

Peaceful protest – A nonviolent gathering of people to peacefully protest something.

Preindustrial – Referring to a period of time before the start of the Industrial Revolution.

Privilege – An advantage, benefit, or immunity certain groups of people or an individual has.

Rewilding – Conservation focused on allowing and encouraging nature to restore itself back to its natural state before humans altered it.

Social justice – The fair distribution of opportunities, privileges, and wealth in society.

Tipping point – A critical point that, if reached, will lead to significant and often irreversible changes.

United Nations – The one place where all nations in the world can gather together to discuss problems and work out solutions that benefit humanity.

ARTIST BIOGRAPHIES

Natasha Donovan is a Métis illustrator with a focus on comics and children's illustration. She has illustrated several award-winning children's books, including *Borders* by Thomas King, *The Sockeye Mother* by Brett D. Huson, *Classified* by Traci Sorell, and *Surviving the City* by Tasha Spillett-Sumner. She has a degree in anthropology from the University of British Columbia, and has worked in academic and magazine publishing. She currently lives in Bellingham, Washington.

Gloria Félix is a Mexican/Purépecha artist and children's book illustrator born and raised in Michoacán, México. Her culture and family are some of her biggest inspirations when it comes to art. After studying animation, Gloria moved to San Francisco to get her MFA in visual development. Gloria has over eight years of experience making art for the animation industry. Her hobbies include walking, life drawing, plein air painting, and eating delicious food with her friends. Currently she lives and paints in Guadalajara.

Ann Maulina is a comic artist from Indonesia. Her original comic is *Raruurien* (raruurien.com). She also works as a freelance comic book artist for Marvel and DC Comics. She holds a bachelor's degree in visual communication design, which gives her a high advantage with art and design projects. She enjoys creating art while exploring some dynamic and harmonic colors.

Bill Masuku is an award-winning comic book and storyboard artist from Zimbabwe. Masuku is the creator of *Captain South Africa*, *Razor-Man*, and *Welcome to Dead World*. As an author Masuku has written in the urban fantasy genre with his novellas *Misfortunism* and *Psychophagy*, books centered on mental health as a form of magic gone awry. He offers his experience in the field of African comic books to guest lecture a fourth-year digital arts course at the University of the Witwatersrand in Johannesburg, South Africa.

Teo DuVall is a queer Chicanx comic artist and illustrator based in Seattle, Washington. They graduated in 2015 with a BFA in cartooning from the School of Visual Arts and have had the immense pleasure of working with Levine Querido, HarperCollins, Dark Horse, Chronicle Books, Scholastic, and more. He has a passion for fantasy, aesthetic ghost stories, and witches of color, and loves being able to create stories for a living. Teo lives with his spouse, their two pets—a giant, cuddly pit bull and a tiny, ferocious cat—and a small horde of houseplants.

Derick Brooks is an illustrator and author from Virginia who loves to create adventurous stories about Black folks. He is currently hard at work on various projects, including his debut graphic novel about intergalactic thumb wrestling called *Grip Up!*

Shivana Sookdeo is an Eisner and Ignatz Award–winning cartoonist and senior designer. Her work is about the personal—everything from body politics to deepest fears. She has been featured in *Elements: Fire*, *Dirty Diamonds*, and *Sweaty Palms*, among others. She lives in Brooklyn and is currently working on a graphic novel and picture book series.

Devon Holzwarth is an award-winning picture book illustrator, author, and painter. Born in Washington, DC, Devon grew up in Panama surrounded by nature and her dad's art supplies. She has lived in many other places over the years but currently calls Germany home, along with her husband, two kids, a galgo dog from Spain, and a little dachshund from Romania.

Anoosha Syed is a Pakistani Canadian character designer and the illustrator of over twenty books, including *I Am Perfectly Designed* by Karamo Brown, APALA honor book *Bilal Cooks Daal* by Aisha Saeed, and her author/illustrator debut, *That's Not My Name!* Some of her past clients include Netflix, Disney, Target, and Google. In her free time, Anoosha hosts a YouTube channel dedicated to free and accessible art and business education for aspiring illustrators. She lives in Toronto with her husband and cat.

Erin Hunting is an Australian illustrator who has drawn comics for *Garfield*, *Archie*, and *The Loud House*. She has also illustrated picture books for Penguin Random House and Insight Editions, and created character designs for Nickelodeon, Grumpy Cat, Tegan and Sara, and Sesame Workshop. Away from her desk she enjoys drawing with copic markers, hanging out with her cat, Louie, reading, and collecting vinyl toys.

Margarita Kukhtina is a children's book illustrator currently based in Batumi, Georgia. She studied fine art at the State Academy of Slavic Culture. She creates illustrations for picture books, advertising, magazines, and posters.

Jade Zhang is a queer Chinese Canadian illustrator and comic artist based in Toronto. She is interested in telling stories about magic, memory, and monsters with feelings. Jade is currently illustrating *Ghost Circus*, a middle grade graphic novel filled to the brim with mystery and ghosts. Previous published works include "How to Survive a Haunting" with the *Shades of Fear* anthology, and *Jim Henson's The Storyteller: Tricksters* with BOOM! Studios.

Natasha Nayo is a 2D animator and illustrator from Ghana with a BFA in animation/illustration from Maryland Institute College of Art. She does character design, visual development, and 2D animations. Her videos were displayed in various festivals such as Encounters Film Festival; Bristol, 2018; and DISCOP Johannesburg, 2019. Her love for creating personal, vibrant comics dates back to 2012. *Drawn to Change the World* is her first published anthology feature.

Victoria Maderna and *Federico Piatti* are Argentinian artists based in Spain. A married couple, they work individually as illustrators creating artwork for books, magazines, and tabletop games, and they make comics in collaboration. They're currently working on Hematite, a graphic novel series about a teenage vampire published by Dargaud (France), which they write and draw together.

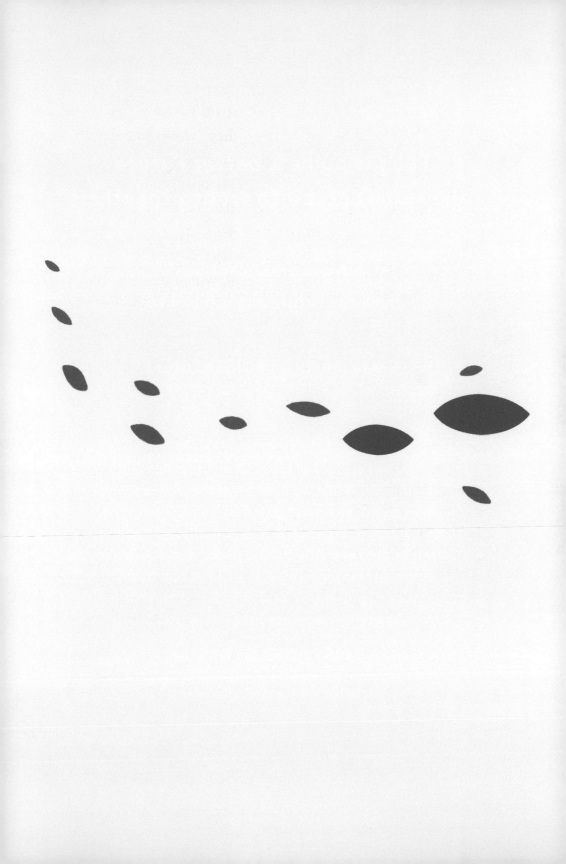

Let's imagine a better future
and manifest it into reality together!

Can you draw what you
think the future might look like?

Share it with us #DTCTWFuture

"We've got loads of ideas for solar panels and
microgrids. While we have all of these pieces, we
don't have a picture of how they come together to
build a new world. For too long, the climate fight has
been limited to scientists and policy experts. While
we need their skills, we also need so much more.
When I survey the field, it's clear that what
we desperately need is more artists."

—MARY ANNAÏSE HEGLAR
Climate justice writer, cohost, and cocreator
of the *Hot Take* podcast and newsletter

PRAISE FOR
DRAWN TO CHANGE THE WORLD

"The world comes together in this call-to-action book about young climate activists. It brilliantly pairs the art of comic illustrators with the inspiring stories of children and teens, including those from LGBTQ+, Indigenous, neurodiverse, disabled, and other marginalized groups, who speak their truths to power and fight for the planet we share."

—SUSAN HOOD,
author of *The Last Straw: Kids vs. Plastics*

"An inspired reminder to listen to the voices of the youth."

—LILY WILLIAMS, coauthor and illustrator
of the Eisner Award–nominated *Go with the Flow*

"You can change the world, and these real-life stories show you just how far you can go with an idea, passion, and the support of your community."

—VICTORIA YING,
author of *City of Secrets* and *Hungry Ghost*

"An approachable, warm, and informative visual guide to climate change activism."

—LAUREN JAMES,
founder of the Climate Fiction Writers League

"A revolution in a book."

—K. A. REYNOLDS,
author of *Izzy at the End of the World*

"One of the many things this graphic novel does superbly is help to decolonize the fight against global warming. It sheds light on the activists from all around the world and how climate change affects their communities and how they step up to make a change."

—DAPO ADEOLA,
award-winning author and illustrator of *Hey You!*

"Not just another climate change book, *Drawn to Change the World* is a fresh, hard-hitting, and personal look at how environmental change has affected and galvanized young people across the globe. It will leave you feeling shocked, inspired, and desperate to make a change."

—DR. JESS FRENCH,
author of *What a Waste*

"Many inspiring voices, lots of incredible illustrations, one important message . . . it's time to change."

—LEISA STEWART-SHARPE,
author of bestselling children's books with the BBC

"Some people say that we should study to become climate scientists so that we can 'solve the climate crisis.' But the climate crisis has already been solved. We already have all the facts and solutions. All we need to do is to wake up and change."

—Greta Thunberg

"You cannot get through a single day without having an impact on the world around you. What you do makes a difference, and you have to decide what kind of difference you want to make. I chose to fight for our planet."

—Jane Goodall

"Climate activists are sometimes depicted as dangerous radicals. But the truly dangerous radicals are the countries that are increasing the production of fossil fuels. Investing in new fossil fuels infrastructure is moral and economic madness."

—António Guterres

Secretary-General of the United Nations

"It is the goal of oppressive systems to make us feel hopeless, to take away our joy, to steal our imagination. And imagination is such a powerful tool, it's not childish or irrelevant: it is actually one of our greatest solutions to imagining a more sustainable, equitable future."

—Wanjiku "Wawa" Gatheru

Founder of Black Girl Environmentalist